This special First Edition of

STORMS OF PERFECTION

VOLUME IV

is signed by author Andy Andrews.

The Edition is limited to 1000 copies

of which 250 are for sale in the

United States of America.

This copy is number __214__ of the First Edition.

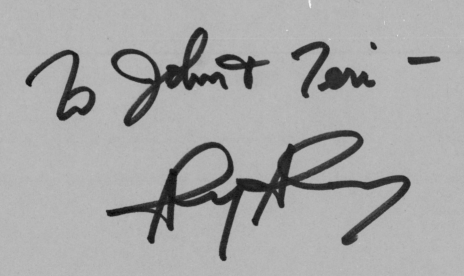

STORMS OF PERFECTION

VOLUME IV

STORMS OF PERFECTION

VOLUME IV

ANDY ANDREWS

Books are available at quantity discounts to schools, civic organizations, corporations, and small businesses. For information, please write to: Marketing Division, Lightning Crown Publishers, P.O. Box 17321, Nashville, TN 37217.

Published in Nashville, Tennessee
by Lightning Crown Publishers
P.O. Box 17321, Nashville, TN 37217.

The Bible verses used in this publication are from the
New American Standard Version and the New King James Version.
Used by permission.

Printed in the United States of America.

FIRST EDITION
First Printing: October 1997

Library of Congress Catalog Card Number: 97-074325
ISBN 0-9629620-7-4

Editor: Robert D. Smith
Book Design: Payne Art Design
Cover Illustration and Layout: Brian Dominey

LIGHTNING CROWN PUBLISHERS

P.O. Box 17321 • Nashville, TN 37217
1-800-726-2639

The following letters are completely the work of historical fiction. Although great pains were taken to research each letter for its historical accuracy and, where possible, to use the recorded signature of each "author," no claim is made that these letters represent the actual writings of the individuals presented in this book. We hope you enjoy this collection for what it is: an attempt to capture the thoughts, ideas, and essence of some of our world's greatest leaders, thinkers, heroes, and difference-makers as they weathered their storms of perfection.

TABLE OF CONTENTS

PREFACE

I was seven years old, barely keeping pace as my father strode purposefully through the woods, the dry brush crackling under our feet. August was rarely pleasant in the deep South, but this year had been especially hot; especially dry.

Walking the densely forested stand of timber that day, young as I was, I was acutely aware of my father's mood. The month-long drought our area was experiencing had him worried. I watched in silence as he broke dry twigs from seemingly lifeless trees and examined the wilting, dull color of the new growth under them. We hiked through the dust of the parched creek bed, following it to the beaver pond where our family often came for picnics. The pond was nearly empty and the beaver lodge, usually a site of frantic activity, stood abandoned on dry land.

Without warning, the wind shifted. With the change in direction came a rapid increase in velocity and a perceptible drop in temperature. It became cool within a matter of seconds, as the wind, whistling above, threatened to send branches crashing down around us. Lightning and thunder worked the atmosphere almost simultaneously, creating explosions of light and sound that terrified me. My father, his arms wrapped around me tightly, was also afraid...and grateful.

He was grateful for this violent performance of nature and the hope of water that came with it. As the trees bent with the wind and the thunder covered my cries, my father sat down, pulled me into his lap, and said, "Don't worry. You'll be all right. Something good is going to come out of this. Be still. Be patient."

As he comforted me, the rain came. Not with the gentle drops I had seen in the past, but in wild, silver sheets bursting all around us. It wound through the limbs and leaves, over rocks, and deep into the tangled thickets, leaving nothing untouched.

And then, as suddenly as it had begun, it was over. The thunder and lightning and wind and rain were gone, their energy exhausted. It was still again, but even at my young age, I noticed a difference. The forest wasn't just still...it was calm.

With his hands, my father wiped the drops of water from my face. Only my deep sobs betrayed the presence of tears, not raindrops, on my cheeks. Then he smiled, wrung out the front of his shirt, and motioned toward the pond. "It'll fill back up now," he said, "and those beavers will be able to spend the winter here like they'd planned."

We turned in time to see a doe and her fawn drinking from the already flowing creek. The frogs had started their own chorus as we headed for home. "Ahh," my father breathed deeply, "everything just smells clean, doesn't it?" And it did. The very air, which only a short time ago had been hot and dirty, now seemed almost sweet. "Let's sit down by this big oak, Son," he said quietly. "I have something to tell you."

I snuggled in beside him, and in very nearly a whisper, he began. "You know," he said, watching me from the corner of his eye, "you weren't the only one scared a little while ago. Those deer were afraid, too. The squirrels huddled together as close as they could get, and what with all the crashes and booms, well, I'm pretty sure the rabbits were worried. But now, something important has happened. The very event that frightened everyone in the forest turned out to be exactly what they needed."

"Do you hear the birds?" I nodded. "Remember how quiet they were before the rain? Now they're hopping around, chirping, drinking from puddles, and feasting on the worms that come out only when the ground is wet. The fish in the pond have more oxygen to breathe and cooler water to swim in. The dust that was on all the plants has been washed away so they are much cleaner for the rabbits and deer to eat. Nobody likes dirty food."

"In fact, Son, all of us are better off now than we were an hour ago. Just because of the storm. What looked like the worst—turned out to be the best. It was a storm of perfection."

●　　●　　●

My dad has been gone for well over a decade, but I can remember that day in the woods as if it happened this morning. Writing this now, I couldn't begin to count the instances I've had reason to recall his words. There have been many storms in my life; and some were more terrifying than that day when I was seven. I do try, however, to keep my father's lesson in my heart. And it is easy to hear him tell me, "Don't worry. You'll be all right. Something good is going to come out of this. Be still. Be patient. It's only a storm of perfection."

ACKNOWLEDGMENTS

Thank you to my wife, Polly, and my manager, Robert D. Smith, who both played an important and critical part in the areas of encouragement, instruction, and inspiration.

My sincere gratitude to Shane Ray, whose consistency, self-discipline, and tact kept me on the straight and narrow and this project on time.

Special acknowledgment to David Hamburg for his expertise and brilliant editing.

Special thanks to Alejandra Galindo, Isabel Galindo, Sandie Dorff, Patrick McCurley, and Chad Poindexter for their creative input in all phases of this production.

My sincere appreciation goes to those whose research and creative skills helped bring the "letter writers" back to life: Katrina Anderson, Diana Barth, Scottie Dayton, Alejandra Galindo, Jeff Gilliam, David Hamburg, Beez Homeyer, Susie Huelsing, Nicole Johnson, Max Reed, and Brian Williams.

Grateful acknowledgment is expressed to Lucy Andrews, Joey Alvarez, Michael Harrison, Carson Poindexter, Tim & Connie Foley, Ellis & Doraine Lucas, Bubba & Sandy Pratt, John & the lovely Elizabeth Parker, and Dexter & Birdie Yager for their encouragement and belief in this project.

Author's Note

The idea of a storm in one's life having value was planted in my mind years ago as a small boy. The *Storms of Perfection* book series was inspired during a discouraging time in my adult life. I wondered why I had only heard the victory stories of successful people. Had they ever gone through rejection, heartache, and depression? Had anyone ever asked them that question?

Storms of Perfection I, II, and *III* contained actual letters from real, live people who had become very successful in a variety of fields. General Norman Schwarzkopf, Joan Rivers, and Norman Vincent Peale were among the 156 total people who participated in the books. Astronauts, sports heroes, and business professionals wrote letters in their own words, on their own stationery, with their own signature at the bottom. The letters told the story of the biggest problem or worst rejection they suffered before becoming successful.

I was shocked at how difficult it actually was to obtain these letters. For the first book, I was turned down by more than 600 people before I reached my goal of 52 letters. That process took almost two years! I was certain that with a completed, successful book in hand, the second book would be easier to compile. It wasn't. To get 52 letters, I was turned down by 458 people. I was ready for the process by the time I had begun book III. Sure enough, I had to wade through more than 1,000 people telling me "no" to find 52 who said "yes." It became funny, actually—I was writing a book about rejection and being taught a lesson about it!

This book, however, was different. *Storms of Perfection IV* became a collection of imaginary letters from the past. Vast research was done to ensure the accuracy of the stories included in the letters, but obviously, literary license was taken regarding the stationery and tone of the letters themselves.

I hope you enjoy this collection of inspirational correspondence, imaginary though it may be, between 52 successful men and women from the past and me. I only wish we'd had the opportunity to speak with them personally. Fortunately, through these pages, they speak to us all.

Andy Andrews
Gulf Shores, Alabama

Foreword

Imagine a magical doorway leading to the secrets of men and women who have literally changed the course of history. A step beyond that threshold would reveal the methods and tactics these world changers used to make their monumental contributions. How much would a peek through such a door be worth? Would we take the time to look? Would we make the effort to study carefully the footsteps of destiny? Or would we turn away, thinking "we are not like these heroes"?

Andy Andrews has opened such a door with *Storms of Perfection IV*. Just as he assembled stories from contemporary success in the previous three *Storms* volumes, Andy Andrews has reached into the pages of history to create a living document that communicates important truths about the human condition. Most of us know that Beethoven was a genius-level musical innovator and that he lived his final days unable to hear his own accomplishments. But we are unaware of struggles early in life that he bravely conquered to put himself in the position to contribute. Most of us don't know that Albert Einstein's first teachers, who, when young Albert was still a tender child, told the boy and his parents that he was a dullard and would not finish his education. In fact, as I read the little-known, historically true accounts that underpinned the successes related in history books, I realized the gift that Andy had given us.

These historical figures are exactly like us today. With all the same challenges, fears, obstacles, and dreams. Therefore, today, we can accomplish great things, just as they have in the past. You see, there is one common thread delicately weaving its way through every story. It is the thread of persistence. A willingness to continue to take action, even when the end is not in sight.

I would like to make a suggestion to all who open the cover of *Storms of Perfection IV*. Do so with the knowledge that you are, in fact, opening the magical door....you are being granted access to the secrets of heroes...and, if you do not look away, you will walk among them.

Congressman Bob McEwen
U.S. House of Representatives

*Dedicated to the memory of Misty Hamlett
and Dr. Joseph H. Huelsing.
Their attitudes and courage continue to
be an example to us all.*

Helen Keller

"AUTHOR"

*…was deaf and blind
from the age of nineteen months.
Having overcome considerable physical
handicaps, she serves as an
inspiration to many.*

1880–1968

What is sometimes more awe inspiring than an individual's remarkable feat of overcoming her handicaps is the humbleness of spirit which she displays afterward. Helen Keller was this kind of person. She could have waved her own banner and have no one to shame her for it. Helen was a sweet, spirited young girl locked in a dungeon of darkness and silence, but the truest of treasures was waiting behind those invisible walls. The quest for this treasure was a lonesome venture. Its way was not charted on any map. Indeed, no one had ever been there before to record the route. This wealth, found in the person of Helen Keller, had to be discovered by methods never before employed.

There were so many reasons for Helen Keller to be hopeless. There were too many barriers and no apparent way out of the darkness. The mere possibility that she could ever come to the point of actually communicating with and understanding the world outside is incredible. It took an amazing amount of courage and determination for her. But Helen Keller went beyond just this. She became a lady of great poise, distinction, and humility, and she gave the credit for her success to her teacher. Indeed, a great deal of credit is due there, but Helen Keller's determination to overcome remains an inspiration to us all.

HELEN KELLER

Mr. Andy Andrews
P.O. Box 2761
Gulf Shores, Alabama 36547

Dear Mr. Andrews,

I was born in Tuscumbia, Alabama, on June 27, 1880, a normal child. Nineteen months later, I was stricken with an illness which left me deaf and blind. Because I was deaf, I became mute.

The condition of my mind was in doubt. Some said I was an idiot. My parents did not believe it, but they could not disprove it. No one could reach me and, thus cut off, I became a phantom living in a world that was a no-world.

I stayed in this world for five years, without hope of leaving it until my mother, casually reading a newspaper, learned of the Perkins Institution for the Blind in Boston. She read about the success a doctor had achieved with one of his patients. Unfortunately, this success had occurred fifty years earlier, and no one had since been able to duplicate the results.

My mother made inquiries and was promised a teacher. On March 3, 1887, my new teacher arrived in Tuscumbia, but my parents' hopes were dashed. The teacher was only twenty-one years of age and had recently graduated from the Perkins Institution herself. She, too, was almost totally blind. Her name was Annie Sullivan.

She began at once spelling with her hand into mine, suiting the word to the action, the action to the word. I responded by imitating the finger motions like a bright, inquisitive animal. It took her a month to reach my mind.

On April 5, my phantom self made contact with reality. While Annie Sullivan pumped water over my hand, it came to me in a flash that water, wherever it was found, was water, and that the finger motions I felt on my palm meant water and nothing else.

In that thrilling moment, I knew that everything had a name and that I had a way to learn those names. I then formed a question by pointing to Annie Sullivan. On my palm she replied, "Teacher."

Mine is actually a story of two lives and the storm in one that brought about a perfection in the other. If it is true, as people say, that I have been an inspiration to millions, then it is Annie Sullivan who deserves the credit. And it is important to note that she was in a position to guide, teach, and help me only because of her own blindness.

Could it be that our Creator, years before I was born, looked at a baby Annie Sullivan and said, "You will have the strength to measure up to this challenge. The way you make use of this challenge will affect humanity for generations to come. You are special to me, and one day you will realize that your blindness was not a curse. It was a gift."

I close, Mr. Andrews, with this thought. With what situation in your life are you struggling? As you learn from your storm, as you defeat it—does your victory make you stronger? Does your victory inspire others and lead them to victories of their own? The question is then: Is your storm a curse . . . or a gift?

Sincerely,

Helen Keller

Helen Keller

Humphrey Bogart

"ACTOR"

*...achieved success in gangster
and tough-guy roles. Some of his most
famous films include* The Maltese
Falcon, Casablanca, *and*
The African Queen.

1899–1957

Who can forget the famous scene in the picture *To Have and Have Not,* when Lauren Bacall teaches Bogie how to whistle? It's no wonder that the movie industry of today is trying to recapture the magic of those older films. Humphrey Bogart is an American classic. He has probably been imitated more than any other actor. His film characters such as Sam Spade, Rick Blaine, Duke Mantee, and Fred C. Dobbs, to name just a few, have become woven into the fabric of American culture. Bogie became a household name and an American icon with his aloof and rugged portrayals on camera.

Bogart's memorable on-screen fights with Cagney, Robinson, and Raft were often small affairs compared with his true-life hardships. Even if you were to watch the more than fifty films that Bogie made, you would still not be able to gain insight into the real man as you will in this short letter. Even the great Bogart dealt with real heartache and difficulties. Perhaps it is what made him such a talented actor.

H U M P H R E Y   B O G A R T

Mr. Andy Andrews
P.O. Box 2761
Gulf Shores, Alabama 36547

Dear Andy,

As you are an entertainer yourself, I feel that I am writing to a comrade. Perhaps you can understand better than most how difficult life can be at times in the public's goldfish bowl. Yours is an interesting concept, to inspire people to consider what "famous people" were like before anyone knew their name. To help others understand that no one is simply granted the keys to success, but that nothing of value comes without great exertion of one's own will, is a mission worthy of your efforts. I have no dignified testimony other than perhaps to reveal that I am no exception to the rule.

People remember me from my roles in the movie business, and as one of America's "tough guys." It's an image that was created for me, an image Americans needed to see portrayed in the motion picture industry during World War II. In reality, however, I was simply an actor. I never got into a real fight in my entire adult life. Truly, I was rough around the edges, and my personality lent itself well to the facade of being tough. But I wasn't the "standard of American male virility" that the movies depicted. I enjoyed practical jokes and socializing with close friends.

After my good fortune of making several movies, many of which now have become American classics, I found myself the subject of a social phenomenon. The "Bogie" persona became the style of the day. In the fashionable circles of society, it had become popular to dress, talk, and display attitudes like Bogie. I sometimes found myself in public being confronted by men I didn't know who wanted to fight with me to show that they could beat up the famous Bogie. I was real, but few people knew Humphrey Bogart. They knew Duke Mantee, Sam Spade, or some other tough-guy role I had played. But as an actor, I had truly been a success in the public's eyes.

Ironically, few people knew during the height of my fame what formidable obstacles, disappointments, and life tragedies I had experienced prior to basking in the limelight. While this tough guy seemed to hold the world by the tail, I still knew where I had come from.

My parents were wealthy. My mother actually made about three times the annual wage of my father, who was a physician. My mother sketched scenes and illustrations for a number of popular magazines near the turn of the century. She was a leader in the early women's suffrage movement. Though my home had an abundance of money, it held little love or affection. My family was held together for the sake of propriety. My mother resented my father because he did not make at least as much money as she did. She felt he was lazy and allowed her to carry the burden of financially supporting the family. My father became addicted to the morphine he carried in his doctor's bag.

My father decided I was to be a surgeon. When I was still in grammar school, my parents decided that I would go to Yale, and so I was sent to a posh school when I was fourteen in preparation for college. But I always liked stirring up things, needling authority. I guess I inherited it from my parents. They needled everyone, including each other. I met a boyhood friend at school, and we amused ourselves by attending theaters and silent motion pictures. It was at this time, during the first World War, that I began my love affair with the movies. I also had a burning desire to enlist in the Navy when I got old enough.

When it was time to move on to the Andover Academy for high school-aged boys, I had no heart to follow the direction my parents had planned for me. I continued in my mischievous ways, including dunking a professor's head in a decorative fountain. Not too surprisingly, I was permanently expelled from school, and my parents' dream of my being a surgeon was dashed. I was not allowed to have dreams of my own. I came home from Andover to endure my mother's constant attempts to shame me. My parents made it abundantly clear to me that I had wasted every chance that could be given, and that I had failed not only myself, but them as well.

I enlisted in the Navy. The Navy got me away from home and the sarcastic needling of my mother about what a ne'er-do-well I was. On one occasion my naval ship was shelled by a U-boat. A splinter of wood from a burst pierced my upper lip, I sustained nerve damage, and my lip was left partly paralyzed. Worse, it made me talk with a slight lisp. I did not know then that these physical handicaps were later to become some of my most advantageous traits as an actor. While playing gangster roles, the scar and the lisp seemed very sinister. No one could duplicate it, and it was enormously popular in films.

After the war, I went home. But though the world was now at peace, there was no peace at home. I returned to my mother constantly belittling me, pointing out what I already knew too well myself—I had little education and no way of earning a living. To my mother, I was typical of every other man: good for nothing that I could take pride in. I renewed my acquaintance with my old schoolmate, whose father was a movie producer. My mother told me that actors were socially unacceptable people. Nevertheless, I took his job offer as a stagehand.

Hindsight is truly 20/20, Andy. I wish I could go back and do so many things differently. Through a series of circumstances too long to list, I found myself acting in very small bit parts on stage. I married young to an actress, more for our career enhancement than for love. It lasted less than a year. My second marriage was marred by violence while I fell into drinking too heavily. The Great Depression hit America, and no one went to see plays anymore. I took an offer to go to Hollywood to act in a movie version of a play I had performed in. My second marriage fell apart. I played meaningless roles in several B-rated movies while nearly starving to death. But I wanted to be an actor. I persisted.

It was only by the good favor of a faithful actor friend of mine, Leslie Howard, that I got the part as Duke Mantee in the picture *Petrified Forest*. It was a huge success, and I became a noted actor with opportunities to play more and bigger roles. Even my parents began to show an interest and said they were proud of me. You may find it ironic, but even after several motion pictures, I only got the leading roles in movies like *Casablanca* and *The Maltese Falcon* after having been rejected several times for the parts. I was not even close to being the first choice for these roles.

In fact, I had been rejected so many times for so many movies that I had come to expect rejections in abundance before landing a good role. I wound up being Warner Brothers' fifth choice to star in *Casablanca*, after their fourth choice, Ronald Reagan, refused to take it.

I married Lauren Bacall, after our shared motion picture, *Casablanca*. We had a wonderful relationship and family. I had finally attained my dream. The victory would not have tasted so sweet without the struggles I endured to reach it. I learned very much in my hard times. I found that character is the most important trait a man can possess. Keep it and you will find happiness. Lose it, and you've lost everything. I can now review my life and find a happy ending. It feels good. And like any good movie, the tough guy wins out in the end over the rough times. You've given me a chance to remember my life as it might have been captured on film. As I rewind the projector to set up the film once more, I find myself repeating, "Play it, Sam!"

Sincerely,

Humphrey Bogart

Jesse Owens

"ATHLETE"

*…was a gold medalist.
His outstanding achievements and
records have made him one of the most
enduring names in Olympic history.*

1913–1980

Jesse Owens was born James Cleveland Owens, the son of sharecroppers who picked cotton in the fields of Oakville, Alabama. Owens encountered much bigotry as he grew up, but managed to overcome his great economic and social disadvantages by attending Ohio State University after his parents moved to Cleveland, and then training diligently in track-and-field for his ultimate goal, the 1936 Olympics, which were held in Berlin. On May 25, 1935, Owens set three world records (in the 220-yard dash, the 220-yard low hurdles, and the running broad jump) and tied another (in the 100-yard dash). He frustrated Adolf Hitler in Berlin by winning three gold medals and sharing in a fourth. Owens wrote an autobiographical saga, *Blackthink: My Life as Black Man and White Man*, in 1970, in which he spoke frankly on the issue of race relations.

JESSE OWENS

Mr. Andy Andrews
P.O. Box 2761
Gulf Shores, Alabama 36547

Dear Andy,

You won't find Oakville, Alabama, on a map today. Eight miles from Decatur, in the northern part of the state, it was more an invention of a white landowner than a geographical area. My father was a sharecropper. We worked a parcel of land with eight other black families. I lived in a two-room shack with my mother, father, and six brothers and sisters.

I see the storm I endured as the storm of poverty. Some might say it was a storm of bigotry, but I don't think so. Racism is a state of mind— yours and mine. And besides, no one called me nigger until I was seven. That's because an Alabama sharecropper's child in the first World War years almost never saw the white man who owned his every breath. In theory, the Emancipation Proclamation had been a wonderful thing, but in 1915 it was only a theory. The Negro had been set free—free to work eighteen hours a day, free to work land he'd never own. Poverty, not prejudice, was my problem.

There were times we came close to starving. We ate beans and onions, potatoes and onions, and bread and onions. But there was never enough.

We were the "luckiest" family for miles around. My father had been blessed with four sons who had lived. I was the only one who couldn't help. It wasn't because I was too young. I was too sick. Every winter I'd come down with pneumonia. I remember one time, lying in bed for the third winter in a row, coughing blood in that cold cabin. My father could- n't find enough wood to keep the fireplace going. I heard my mother say to my father, "He's going to die. Little J.C. is going to die unless we do something."

Just when we thought things couldn't get worse, they did. Our neighbor about a mile down the road was dead. My father began share- cropping about the same time Joe had. Joe had always treated him like a little brother.

Joe had to work his land alone because his wife kept having stillborn babies. Each time she'd get pregnant, they didn't pray for a son to help in the field, just for something alive. A child would have made life bearable. Yet, the years passed, and all Joe and Betty shared were new gravestones in the back of their house. A new one every twelve months or so.

Then Joe got a "sign." Something told him that Betty would become pregnant again and this time the baby would not only live, but be a son. When her belly began to swell, Joe stopped feeling tired. He worked as never before and whistled every day until the baby came. It came, dead as always. Only this time it took Betsy with it. So Joe Steppart killed himself.

My father changed after that. Not enough to get drunk or abandon us—he never once did either—but he began to think out loud about what was becoming of all of us.

Then the other shoe dropped. On a cool night in February of 1921, the landowner summoned my father. It scared us all because it had never happened before. My father met with an assistant (the landowner never spoke to my father). My father was told that his "deal" was being reworked. He was making too much money. Now he would receive less.

"Less," my father asked? "What about my family?" He was finally losing forty-two years of control. "We worked hard. I want my sons to amount to more than I have."

"Your sons will never amount to anything," the man shouted. "Just be grateful if they survive."

Well, Andy, we survived and we did amount to something. The poverty that seemed to have us so totally beaten became a catalyst for achievement. So many people rarely fulfill their life's potential because they are not forced to think, explore, or stretch.

Poverty was a blessing in a way. I determined to learn, grow, change, and become. Even my sickly childhood held a hidden treasure. As I exercised to increase my lung capacity, I found an aptitude for running and jumping of which I was not aware. The end result of my sickly childhood? Four gold medals at the 1936 Olympic Games.

Every day will be a learning experience. You will miss more than you catch. Things will change fast—change with them. Develop an attitude for the future. Don't exist on what you have done. Exist on what you can do.

Sincerely,

Jesse Owens

"Experience is not what happens to a man,
it is what a man does with what
happens to him."

Aldous Huxley

Albert Einstein

"PHYSICIST"

*...considered one
of the greatest and most popular
scientists of all time. He is best
known for his Theory of Relativity.*

1879–1955

Albert Einstein was born in Ulm, Germany, on March 14, 1879. The young genius spent most of his life in Munich, where his family owned a small electrical machine manufacturing shop. It is interesting to note that Albert did not talk until age three. However, he did exhibit a brilliant curiosity about nature and an ability to understand complex mathematical concepts. In fact, he taught himself Euclidean Geometry at the age of twelve. His family suffered several business setbacks, and when they moved to Milan, Italy, Albert took the opportunity to withdraw from school and spend the year with his family. When he reentered school, he completed his secondary education in Arrau, Switzerland, and then entered the Swiss National Polytechnic in Zurich.

Upon graduation—and because his professors did not think highly of this unconventional young man and would not recommend him for a university position—Einstein worked as a tutor, substitute teacher, and in the Swiss patent office in Bern. Einstein married a university sweetheart, fathered two sons, divorced, and later remarried. He continued to study physics on his own, formulating theory that proved difficult for his contemporaries to accept or even understand. However, in 1905, his Theory of Relativity began gaining attention. Later, in 1919, when a key point was proven true during an eclipse of the sun, Einstein's place in history was secured.

Albert Einstein proved he was more than a mathematician. He was a doorway to greater understanding of our world and our relationship with that world. Winner of the Nobel Prize in physics in 1921, he played a much larger role than simply scientific, until his death in 1955. And in many ways, Albert Einstein still guides modern theory and philosophy today.

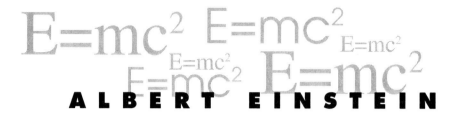

ALBERT EINSTEIN

Andy Andrews
P.O. Box 2761
Gulf Shores, Alabama 36547

Dear Andy,

Storms of Perfection. Quite an interesting choice of words, my friend. I have found in my studies (or more correctly put, in my mental wanderings through lush gardens of imagination) that much of the universe we inhabit appears to be locked in a perpetual, violent storm. However, when understood fully, we find that the storm has purpose, deeper meaning, and is a necessary part of the process of positive creation. I know this to be true in my personal life.

I was born in Ulm, Germany, and grew up in Munich and Milan. I attended university in Zurich at the Federal Institute of Technology and received my doctorate at the University of Zurich in 1905. This led to an appointment at the Prussian Academy of Sciences as the director of theoretical physics and later to a Nobel Prize in 1921 for my work in that discipline. Through all of this, I had to ask, "What is it about me that my peers find so extraordinary?" You see, it is not that I am inordinately smart, it is simply that I stay with problems longer.

At any rate, things seemed to be going well, no? Yet there was a growing darkness in our world. A brooding *storm*, to use your word, Andy, and in 1934 my property was confiscated, taken from me along with my German citizenship. A destructive force was at work in the uniform of the Nazi regime. To be rejected from my homeland because I had been born to a

Jewish family was outrageous. Of course at that time we had no idea of the ultimate horror that the Nazis were capable of unleashing.

So I was forced to rethink my place in the world, to revise my plans, for my home, my boyhood memories, my family history, and my life would most certainly never be connected to Germany again.

I know now that there must have been a reason for this turn of events, for I could never believe that God would play dice with the universe. I spent much time thinking and working through the emotions I felt. Then I realized that throughout history, great spirits have always found violent opposition from mediocre minds. The latter cannot understand it when a man does not thoughtlessly submit to hereditary prejudices but honestly and courageously uses his intelligence.

That same year, I accepted a position at the Institute for Advanced Study at Princeton. Where I would be permitted to follow my intellectual pursuits, where I could revel in an atmosphere of freedom and intellectual stimulation.

America I discovered, was a land that encouraged its people to imagine, and, to me, imagination is even more important than knowledge. Knowledge is limited. Imagination encircles the world. I emerged from "the storm" into a new home, where I could work in peace—not a perfect home, mind you, but a very loving home that encouraged me to formulate and advance my theories, theories that many think to be beyond their understanding. Believe me, they are not. For example, put your hand on a hot stove for a minute, and it seems like an hour. Sit with a pretty girl for an hour, and it seems like a minute. That's relativity!

When we find ourselves in the inevitable storm of life, Andy, I have found a truth: If the solution is simple, God has answered.

Your friend,

A. Einstein

Albert Einstein

"No one can make you feel
inferior without your consent."

Eleanor Roosevelt

Ludwig van Beethoven

"COMPOSER"

*…considered by many
to be the greatest in history.
He wrote symphonies, concertos,
sonatas, and vocal music.*

1770–1827

Ludwig van Beethoven was the second-oldest child of court musician Johann van Beethoven in 1770. Young Ludwig's father drilled him relentlessly in the hopes of showcasing him as a child prodigy. Although bordering on cruel, this early training led to many appearances, beginning at age eight, and eventually to more formal training in Bonn, where Beethoven studied and worked as a musician. In 1787 he was granted a paid leave of absence to travel to Vienna to study under Mozart. Soon, however, he was forced to return to Bonn, where he cared for his family following his mother's death.

Beethoven returned to Vienna in 1792 and began lessons with Haydn, Albrechtsberger, Schenck, and Salieri. His gift for musical improvisation and passion was recognized by nobility, who patronized him, thus allowing him the luxury of living as a freelance composer without financial worry.

Around 1798, Beethoven noticed a deterioration in his hearing. This led him to withdraw from the world and eventually to communicate only by writing in notebooks. After battling a long illness, the greatest composer of the time died on March 29, 1827. More than thirty thousand mourners and curious onlookers were present at the funeral procession.

Beethoven

Mr. Andy Andrews
P.O. Box 2761
Gulf Shores, Alabama 36547

My Friend,

I cannot tell you what this correspondence means to me. I pray that it is understood by you, Andy, and by others who read these words. My time was not a happy time. Yes, there were exciting things occurring across the face of the earth: America was proclaiming her independence, France was fighting for freedom, science and art were joining hands. But, for Ludwig van Beethoven, life was a desperate struggle. I was the oldest of six brothers and sisters, and I watched all but three die as infants. My mother was a gentle, kind, strong woman whom I loved and respected deeply. She was my best friend. My father, though, was of a different nature. Impressed by Amadeus Mozart's rise to popularity and the accompanying "metallic recognition," he set out to make me the provider of his fame and fortune. As his favorite pasttime was drinking, his demands were often as unrealistic as his drunken view of the world. Many times, late at night, returning home after carousing with cronies, he dragged me from my bed determined to beat the music into my head. I practiced for hours on end while other children played outside. I recall standing on the piano stool (for I wasn't yet tall enough to sit and reach the keys), weeping as I played. I came to a point of belief, even then, that there was a reason much larger than myself for the spark of music inside me. It was a spark that would not die.

As I grew and continued to pursue my music, I felt an expanding intuitive knowledge that the spirit of good and beauty were identical. A deep inspiration led me toward an end. I knew not why or where, but it was compelling to the degree of being *irresistible. In this inspiration I found my joy. Wrapped in the warmth of greater meaning, in a place where all concerns of self were left behind, I was truly creative and happy. So it was off to Vienna to study music. After all, Mozart, Haydn, and Gluck were working there. I had one single thought. I must go.*

I shall never forget walking into a production meeting for one of Mozart's operas. The great man was locked into his work, yet received me with cool courtesy. He invited me to play, which I did well, if I may be allowed to say so. The composer obviously thought it was a piece I had practiced exclusively for this meeting and was prepared to casually bid me farewell. I stopped him, however, and asked that he give me a theme on which to improvise. The gauntlet was thrown down! I had never felt so alive. My hands flew over the keys as I developed and embellished and made the piece mine. The master was truly impressed as he turned to a group of friends assembled in an adjoining room and said, "Keep an eye on this young man! The world will hear from him someday!" Mozart's encouraging words quenched a raging thirst inside me. It seemed my life was beginning to take shape. And then I received urgent word from home. My dear mother had fallen ill. I must return at once.

I lost my mother and baby sister within weeks. My best friend, my foothold in this world, gone. My father and younger brothers were unable to deal with the loss. At the age of seventeen, it was up to me to see to the arrangements. The hurt of selling my mother's clothes and possessions to secondhand dealers to cover expenses will never subside. I felt I was selling the last attachment to anything I loved in this life. And then I realized the truth. Though I seemed to have nothing left, I had everything in my grasp. For my understanding of goodness and beauty could be expressed through the one thing that could never be taken from me—my music.

Back in Vienna, I studied under Haydn, focused on learning the rules of the day and expanding music into new uncharted areas. I met opposition, of course. What I was doing broke the rules! But in the opposition I detected a grudging admiration for my work. Ever so slight. Never to be fully enjoyed in my lifetime. Yet I knew somehow that my music would reach beyond Ludwig van Beethoven, and that the glow of acceptance would someday explode into a raging fire of acknowledgment. This realization gave me the freedom to compose as I heard the music. Regardless of the rules of the day, I had been granted immunity from a source beyond all contemporary understanding. I knew that I was close to God in those times. I knew that I created for the future. I find it almost amusing that as I drew closer to the infinite, I could hear less and less the clatter of the world I had struggled through.

The deterioration of my hearing could be called my final storm, Andy. I recall writing to a friend:

> "How can I, a musician, say to people, 'I am deaf!' I
> shall, if I can, defy this fate, even though there will be times
> when I shall be the unhappiest of God's creatures I
> live only in music . . . frequently working on three or four
> pieces simultaneously."

Perhaps this was the completion of my maturing in this life. As my hearing left me, I could no longer perform as a virtuoso pianist. That left me to compose only as a means to release the music. I saw few people as I lived out my days. My new compositions were not widely popular because they did not follow contemporary guidelines. As I took my walks about Vienna, I would hear the rhythm in my head, and as I worked out the piece mentally, I found myself beating the time with my arms. More than once I looked up to see the citizens of Vienna laughing at what must have appeared to be a madman. My clothing was old and tattered, my hearing was totally gone, my finances were nonexistent. As I composed my final works, I perceived I was totally alone.

This, Andy, is my deepest hope. That you and your friends understand what I now know as fact. Do not read this letter and think, "Poor Ludwig." Know instead that the greater the intensity of the storms in one's life, the brighter and warmer the sun shines at the finale of the tempest. My entire life could be called a succession of turbulent storms. I had dark, despairing times. And even though I perceived myself to be alone in my last days on earth, tens of thousands of people my music had touched were there to send me on my way. Now, from my vantage point, with the luxury of a wider vision, the effect my music has had in the world makes the storms I suffered seem a small price to pay to have married good and beauty with the lives of so many.

As a young man, full of bravado, I wrote: "I shall never crawl—my world is the universe."

And now I pass that banner to you. See your way through the storms and join me in the warmth of a greater genius that beams like a far-off sun.

With love,

C. V. Beethoven

Ludwig van Beethoven

"He who sows sparingly will also reap sparingly,
and he who sows bountiful will
also reap bountiful."

II Corinthians 9:6

Joan of Arc
"HEROINE"

...united the nation of France. She turned the Hundred Years' War in France's favor.

1412–1431

What if, instead of Washington, Grant, Lee, Pershing, MacArthur, and Schwarzkopf, we acclaimed a teenage girl as one of our great military leaders? Seems strange, doesn't it? Yet that is precisely the legacy which Joan of Arc has left for the French people.

She was born, we believe, in 1412 in Domrémy, France. Her parents, James and Zabet, were farmers. Joan lived the life of a typical young girl until she was thirteen. It was then that she first heard her famous "voices," telling her she must go to fight for the Dauphin of France against the occupational army of England. It was there that Joan enjoyed her finest hour. She became a heroine and a symbol for the people of France.

Unfortunately, political intrigue led to her downfall. Captured in Toulon by the English, she was turned over to the Inquisition and tried for heresy at Rouen. With the outcome determined long before her trial began, she was found guilty and burned at the stake in 1431, when she was only nineteen years of age.

Fortunately, Joan's legacy of courage and determination lives on. Her image was used to rally the French people to victory in World Wars I and II, and her name alone inspires us still.

Joan of Arc

Mr. Andy Andrews
P.O. Box 2761
Gulf Shores, Alabama 36547

Mr. Andrews,

In the Apostle Paul's first letter to Timothy, he says to him, "Don't let anyone look down on you because you are young, but set an example for the believers in speech, in life, in love, in faith and in purity." This is how I tried to live my life. This is how I will face my death as well.

I know it's only a matter of time now. The endless hours of questioning by the inquisitors, the insinuations that I was either a witch or a whore or both; all have ceased. The sentencing was swift and to the point: "I sentence thee to be burned upon the stake." All that is left now is the wait.

I imagine I should be angry or panicked. My thoughts should be on the political games that brought me to this place; a king who no longer had the will to fight and would instead trade me to appease a duke; a duke who would trade a military trial for a religious one to appease the Inquisition. Perhaps my mind should consider the fate that awaits me. But that is not where my heart is.

Instead, my heart is in my father's garden in Domrémy. I am a young tomboy playing among the flowers. I am thirteen when I first hear the voices, St. Catherine and St. Michael among them. They tell me of God's plan for me. He wants me to fight, for France and the young dauphin who would be king. And so I set out on my quest. I throw my family into an uproar by breaking off my engagement to a young suitor. This resulted in a public suit. To prepare for war, I cut my hair short and wore the clothes of a warrior instead of a farmer girl.

Soon, for better or for worse, I was the talk of my village. Most dismissed me as a madwoman, others as a witch.

An uncle of mine agreed to take me to the governor, the king's representative. He tried to explain the visions I had experienced, but was roughly dismissed as the uncle of a very disturbed young woman. I was sent home in disgrace. I faced the choice we all face when an obstacle blocks our path, to turn our backs on our calling, or to persevere. My calling, my voices, gave me no choice. A second visit to the governor, then a third, finally convinced him to send me to the dauphin at Chinon.

There, when I met the dauphin, momentum and public favor were with me. The dauphin sent me with supply wagons and a few soldiers to relieve Orléans, a town under siege for some six months. I soon found that this was meant to be a political journey rather than a military one, but God had not led me to talk. The people of Orléans rallied around me, and together we proved that a citizenry driven by belief will overcome military might. The English fled, and Orléans was free. Emboldened by the English defeat, the dauphin summoned his courage and traveled to Reims. I stood by his side as God fulfilled His promise that France would again have a king.

These are the thoughts that buoyed my spirit through my king's abandonment of our quest for freedom, my capture, and trial. They bring me a smile even now as I await the executioner's flames. And they will be my final thoughts as I see my Lord's face. We all have our voices, and we all decide whether we will follow them. I have never regretted following mine, despite the pain and the tears, for it is those voices that will lead us to triumph.

With best wishes,

Jehanne

Joan of Arc

"The key to your universe
is that you can choose."

Carl Frederick

General Robert E. Lee

"MILITARY LEADER"

…his genius was probably the single greatest factor in keeping the Confederacy alive through the Civil War.

1807–1870

The American Civil War will always be a bloodstain on the pages of our national history. Both sides of the Mason-Dixon line had their heroes, and some from both sides remain heroes still in the eyes of a reunited nation. Robert E. Lee was the brilliant Confederate general whose military genius was probably the greatest single factor in keeping the Confederacy alive throughout the war. Though enormously outgunned, outmanned, and out-supplied the South held a realistic hope of winning the war, thanks to Lee's savvy as a soldier.

Lee was such a distinguished and recognized military strategist, Abraham Lincoln summoned him personally to Washington, D.C., in order to offer him the field command of the Union forces when war between the states appeared imminent. Lee declined. The rest is obviously history, but it is insightful now to revisit the general in order to understand that one's personal storms may affect our lives much more than perhaps expected.

ROBERT E. LEE

Mr. Andy Andrews
P.O. Box 2761
Gulf Shores, Alabama 36547

Dear Andy,

Even in a democracy, it is not always easy for a country's people to live in harmony. We are all so vastly different. Our political views, the way we dress, even our speech is dissimilar, but for the most part we simply agree to disagree.

There was a time, however, a little more than a hundred years ago, when the people of our country disagreed so bitterly that some felt they could not continue living with the rest. And so, a war was joined. A war between states to determine if we should remain one nation or become two.

I was chosen to lead the army of the South. The war lasted four years. It was a vicious, bloody, miserable four years that pitted friend against friend, brother against brother. I literally directed it all.

At one point, in a series of fields near Gettysburg, Pennsylvania, we engaged the Union Army in a single battle that took the lives of more than 50,000 men. That, incidentally, is more men than died in our country's later involvement in Vietnam. It is not possible to convey to you the horror of that engagement.

I thought I was going to win. I had never failed at anything. Growing up, I had always been first in my class as a soldier and had accomplished every task set before me. I thought I was going to win. I thought I was going to be the man who split the United States right down the middle. I thought I was going to win. Thank God I did not.

The purpose of this letter is to provide a degree of perspective on history that only the passing of 100-plus years can give. When I offer the opinion, "Thank God I did not win," one must understand that I have had a while now to come to that conclusion. Was I happy or even relieved at the defeat? Certainly not, but time does offer a clearer view than I had the day I signed the papers of surrender.

We the United States of America have become the greatest nation in the world. As one united front, we are able to protect our friends, feed the world's hungry, and be a tower of strength to which the weak can turn. We have taken the best of the South, combined with the best of the North, and moved forward as a single entity the likes of which has never been seen in history! And, of course, none of this would have been possible if not for the greatest defeat of my life.

One final word—this on forgiveness and moving on with the future. I saw many a bitter man whose productive life ended the day the war was over. Several came to me with hate in their eyes and said, "Let's not accept this result as final. Let's keep our anger alive. Let's be grim and unconvinced and wear our bitterness like a medal." These men offered to make me their leader in this continuing cause.

I told them no. I had learned long before that forgiveness is a powerful tool for moving on with one's life—more powerful by far for the forgiver! You see, we cannot control whether or not we are forgiven, but we can control the process of forgiving. The process of forgiving brings a new beginning, a new life, and the opportunity to move forward. "Abandon your animosities," I told the men, "and go about the job of making your sons Americans."

Sincerely,

Robert E. Lee

Robert E. Lee

"A man is not finished
when he's defeated;
he's finished when he quits."

Richard Nixon

Noah

"PATRIARCH"

*...responsible for
building the ark referred
to in the book of Genesis.*

Genesis 6–Genesis 9

Nearly every child has grown up with the story of Noah's ark. It is an exciting story and has enormous meaning to us. Can you imagine building a sailing vessel of such enormous proportions in a land where there was not even a body of water large enough to support it? Noah and his three sons built this ship without the advantage of power tools, without anything like sandpaper or nails. There was no lumber supply store or hardware merchants displaying ripping saws for their convenience. Estimates place a time frame of 120 years just to construct the behemoth ark.

One hundred and twenty years is a long time, any way you look at it. But can you picture going about such back-breaking labor while being subjected to the ceaseless humiliating taunts of everyone in your society? That would rival Job's patience...and Noah had the advantage of God Himself supporting his efforts. Still, the burden and responsibility must have been fantastic. I found that Noah had incredible insight and some very valuable advice for us today. And yes, he must have had a sense of humor!

Mr. Andy Andrews
P.O. Box 2761
Gulf Shores, Alabama 36547

Dear Andy,

The ark took me 120 years to build. That's the first thing I want to tell you— 120 years! Most people don't know that. I don't know what they think — maybe it took a year, or that the guys down at the marina used forklifts for the heavy timbers or what — but we built this thing right by ourselves. When I say "by ourselves," I am speaking of my sons, Shem, Ham, Japeth, and me.

It all started with a conversation I had one day with God. I was a farmer. I never had any interest in sailing until He came up with the ark idea. "I want you to build an ark," I think were His exact words.

"What's an ark?" I asked, and He told me.

Then He says, "The ark should be 300 cubits long, 50 cubits wide, and 30 cubits tall."

"What's a cubit?" I asked, and He told me.

God said to finish it with pitch inside and to put one door in the side and to build the ark with three decks. He told me to fill the ark with a male and female of every kind of animal. "And one more thing," He said. "Make sure the ark has a roof, because I'm going to make it rain. A lot."

Well, to make a long story very short, everyone thought I was nuts. We started construction right there on the edge of town. There was no ocean or even a lake for miles around, so "boat" didn't even register in people's minds for a while. Most of them thought it might be a big restaurant or a hotel or something, and they all stood around gawking.

I finally said, "Look, it's a boat, okay? An ark if you want to be specific, and God told me to build it. He's ticked off at the way things have turned out down here, and He's determined to start over with a flood. Anyway, we have only 120 years to get this thing finished, and we're working here with primitive tools. So either go home and leave us alone or pick up one of those rocks and chop down a tree."

Nobody helped. Even the people who were inclined to pitch in were swayed by the attitudes of their friends. Several times I told them that this was an opportunity for everyone. "Anyone who chooses to do the work," I said, "will be rewarded with a place on the ark." Nobody helped.

I might mention here that when the ark began to float after several days of heavy thunderstorms, quite a few of those same people changed their minds, beat on the door, and less than politely requested a seat. It was too late, however. We were in an oversold situation, and God had already sealed the door.

I was reminded of the saying, "Dig your well before you get thirsty." That, I thought, had an application to their situation, however general. Specifically, I did not imagine them thirsty in the least!

Years later, as I told and retold the story to my grandchildren and their grandchildren, I was asked if I had ever doubted the successful outcome of my adventure. And the answer, of course, is no.

My own father, Lemech, was a naysayer. Neighbors rolled their eyes when my name was mentioned, and my family often ate alone at town gatherings. "All Noah seems to talk about," people would say, "is that ark thing."

I never doubted the work, and I never doubted the end result, because I never doubted my decision to build the ark. I never doubted my decision to begin, because it was a decision based on God's guidance. If a project or a business or an activity is begun with God's guidance, then work hard and work consistently — success, with God's timing, is inevitable.

I mentioned God's timing for success. Often, we want results for which we are not ready. God's plans always include a process of personal growth — His way of getting us ready for future success. There were many years enduring the laughter and taunts when I begged God to go ahead and make it rain. God's timing, however, was perfect. The rain started to fall as the last animal walked up the ramp — any earlier would have been a disaster. We simply would not have been ready to handle what God had promised!

One final point, advice, if you will, for those who pray about their decisions. I have always been aggravated with people who say God led them to do this or that. Then when the work is hard or the results don't happen according to their timing, they quit by saying that now God wanted them to do something else.

Here is my advice: If the same God who told me to build a boat in the desert tells you that He has a plan for you, believe it, follow through, and don't be distracted. The process will most likely be difficult, frustrating, and discouraging, but don't quit. Your success, in God's timing, is inevitable. God has told you what to do. His decisions are perfect, and because of that ... God doesn't change His mind!

Sincerely,

Noah

Thomas Jefferson

"PHILOSOPHER/ PRESIDENT"

*...was the
author of the Declaration of
Independence. Later, he became the
third president of the United States.*

1743–1826

Thomas Jefferson left no doubt as to how he wished to be remembered. His epitaph reads: "Author of the Declaration of American Independence and of the Statute of Virginia for religious freedom and Father of the University of Virginia."

Few individuals have exerted as much influence on the course of American history as did Jefferson. His logic and leadership prevented the American Revolution from turning in and destroying itself. He suggested our *e pluribus unum* motto and created the American monetary system—two of his least recognized achievements—and his arguments against a national bank laid the foundation for states' rights by asserting that Congress could not "do anything they please." Jefferson wrote the parliamentary handbook still used by Congress today, created West Point, and is responsible for our two-party system, forming the Democratic-Republican party to oppose the Federalists. Interestingly, the first political party contest for the presidency between John Adams and Jefferson set the vicious tone presidential campaigns have had ever since.

When Jefferson wasn't consumed by politics, he was devoted to science and agriculture. He built a new compact threshing machine to streamline wheat harvesting, and his design to improve the mold-board plow won him a gold medal from the Societé d'Agriculture du Départment de la Seine. Jefferson was president of the nation's preeminent scientific society, the American Philosophical Society. His greatest contribution as a statesman was coaxing Congress to underwrite the Lewis and Clark expedition.

𝔗𝔥𝔬𝔪𝔞𝔰 𝔍𝔢𝔣𝔣𝔢𝔯𝔰𝔬𝔫

Mr. Andy Andrews
P.O. Box 2761
Gulf Shores, Alabama 36547

Dear Mr. Andrews:

A single event wiped away all my plans and left me a blank which I had not the spirits to fill up. It came upon the heels of a disastrous two years in which I, as governor of Virginia, had no real authority or the resources to govern and defend what was then the largest of the states in the newly formed independent confederation. My two terms ended in failure, failure to protect my beloved Virginia from invasion, rape, and destruction, and I returned to Monticello frustrated, disappointed, and facing unsubstantiated charges of cowardice under fire.

When I was elected governor on June 1, 1779, a British naval blockade and rampant inflation were ruining Virginia's economy; she was basically indefensible and under direct threat of military conquest, having never been mobilized for an extended war. Virginia's contribution of men and money to the general cause was so great that there was not a regular within our state nor arms to put into the hands of the militia.

After twenty-two months in an office ill suited to the demands of a state at war, I reached a crossroads on April 15, 1781. On that raw and rainy day at 10:00 a.m., our five-month-old daughter died. Lucy Elizabeth was the third child we lost, and Patty never fully recovered from what was her fifth difficult birth in seven years. She was often ill throughout her confinement, suffering long bouts of depression, and her declining health precipitated my decision to not seek a third term as governor, for public service and private misery are inseparably linked together.

Patty's sixth pregnancy reduced me to such a level of decrepitude that even Cornwallis's surrender (October 19, 1781) could not lift it. What devoted husband would not be so afflicted by overwhelming anxiety upon seeing his devoted wife swollen beyond all reasonable proportions?

At 1:00 a.m. on May 8, 1782, our second Lucy Elizabeth was born, weakening Patty so by the ordeal of delivering the sixteen-pound infant that she never recovered. Thus began my summer of dreadful suspense and the four most terrible months of my life. I watched helplessly, nursing and feeding Patty, reading to her, never out of calling, until she was torn from me at 11:45 a.m. on September 6, 1782. Grief plunged my mind into a stupor which rendered me as dead to the world as she was whose loss occasioned it. I was absolutely unable to attend to anything like business and succumbed to many a violent outburst of sorrow.

My miserable existence was too burthensome to be borne, and were it not for the infidelity of deserting the sacred charge left me, I could not wish its continuance a moment. For what could it be wished? All my plan of comfort and happiness reversed by a single event, and nothing answering in prospect before me but a gloom unbrightened with one cheerful expectation. The care and instruction of our children indeed afforded some temporary abstractions from this wretchedness. My friends rallied to my rescue and, in an effort to draw me away from the scene of my anguish, offered again the commission as one of the ministers plenipotentiary for negotiating a peace with Great Britain in France. In preparing for it and the welfare of my children, I gradually recovered and began to contemplate the distant possibilities of my career.

The school of affliction taught me that for ills so immeasurable, time, silence, and occupation are its only medicines, and these but assuage, they never can suppress the deep drawn sigh which recollection forever brings up, until recollection and life are extinguished together. This world abounds indeed with misery; to lighten its burthen, we must divide it with one another. How grateful is the solace of our friends.

My terms as governor were important to my political education, honed my administrative abilities, and gave me the experience to see the difficulties of this, the greatest of all, the presidency of the United States. They made me determined to adduce every power I could to the Confederacy, to coerce the consolidation of the American states, to force those states into a new compact that would make them more perfect, that would make them one nation. For it is the union of these states that is their palladium of safety, their prosperity and glory.

There are, I acknowledge, even in the happiest life, some terrible convulsions, heavy set-offs against the opposite page of the account. I think that it is a good world on the whole; that it has been framed on a principle of benevolence, and more pleasure than pain dealt out to us. During my fifteen years as legislator, I became the dominant figure and driving force in Congress, wrote thirty-one reports and documents that strengthened and stabilized the American Confederacy, laid the foundation for this country's orderly westward expansion, and developed an uncomplicated coinage system, one of my greatest legislative achievements.

Life is of no value but as it brings us gratifications. My five years as an American diplomat in France and Europe were the watershed of my mature political life. I emerged a respected statesman who returned to the United States with a sophisticated radical worldview that won me two terms as president and enabled me to coordinate one of the great diplomatic coups of all time, bloodlessly doubling the territory of the United States through the Louisiana Purchase. Although my hopes, indeed, sometimes failed, it is through education, self-discipline, and hard work that one advances to self-perfection.

Sincerely yours,

Thomas Jefferson

Buddy Holly

"ENTERTAINER"

...one of the first
major performers of rock 'n' roll music.
His career was cut short when he
died in a plane crash at the age of 22.

1938–1959

As an entertainer, I have seen what a lasting effect people in my profession often have on people all over the world. Mass media have directed worldwide attention to points of interest. And Buddy Holly was a major point of interest in the 1950s, as the younger generation had begun to shed some of its previously held inhibitions. It was a daring time, a period of experimentation and of new things. Rock 'n' Roll was young, and with a nation full of teenage baby boomers, the country itself was young and vivacious.

Buddy Holly was the poster child for the fifties generation. Holding a Fender Stratocaster guitar or snapping his fingers with a wide smile on his face, he portrayed the happiness and spirit then sweeping across America. His music was upbeat and irresistible to us. His sound could not be contained within the borders of America, but was an inspiration to budding English fans as well. Buddy Holly was immensely popular, rivaling even Elvis Presley in audience appeal. He was on the music charts only four short years prior to his death in the airplane crash that also took the lives of rock legends Ritchie Valens and J.P. Richardson, "the Big Bopper." *That'll Be the Day* . . . *Peggy Sue* . . . through his songs and continuing influence, Buddy Holly remains a part of our consciousness even today.

Mr. Andy Andrews
P.O. Box 2761
Gulf Shores, Alabama 36547

Dear Andy,

In 1955 I got my first big break in music, when I was offered a recording contract with Decca Records. At the time, there were three major record companies with country & western divisions in Nashville—Decca, Columbia, and RCA Victor. Columbia was not then interested in rockabilly— RCA Victor had just signed Elvis Presley—but I found a receptive listener in Paul Cohen, Nashville A&R (Artists and Repertoire) director for Decca. With RCA Victor having just signed Elvis, Decca was open to the idea of giving a contract to a similar rockabilly singer.

I was of course elated at the offer and headed off to Nashville. The first thing I was told was that I couldn't use my own musicians and could not play my own rhythm guitar on the sessions. Nor did they think that a rock 'n' roll style of drumming was necessary.

I accepted Decca's decision. I was ready to do whatever was asked of me and whatever it took to get started in the business. After all, Decca was a major label and had been a leader in the country field for years. But that was just the problem. The company and the men who were in charge of my first recordings were involved in country music too deeply and too successfully to cope with rock 'n' roll.

Those first recordings on Decca have since been described as country & western, although that was not what we had intended at the time. They were supposed to appeal to rock 'n' roll audiences as well. This was now 1956, and Elvis was having his first million sellers on RCA Victor, and rock 'n' roll was becoming a national phenomenon! Decca apparently wanted me to be a rockabilly artist along the same lines as Elvis, but my records received little promotion of any sort in any market.

After a long, unsuccessful year, Decca chose not to continue my contract. Truthfully, I was just as happy to be leaving the label. Especially in light of the conversation I had had with Paul Cohen. I'll never forget him telling me that I didn't have the voice to be a singer and should forget about a musical career. According to Norman Petty, the producer who handled most of my future recordings, Cohen called me "the biggest no-talent I have ever worked with."

The advice of those who told me to give up my career only caused me to try harder. So, before long, I rebounded from this discouragement. The association with Decca had been an unhappy one for me. However, looking at it now, in light of my subsequent career, it was actually best that I had failed with Decca. I was to have much more independence with Norman Petty and Coral Records.

Those experiences taught me much about the recording industry and the people involved. I matured as a person and learned a little better how to deal with such problems. Now when anyone feels they can tell me how to run my musical career, I look them straight in the eye and say, "That'll Be the Day!"

Sincerely,

Buddy Holly

Buddy Holly

"The measure of a man is the
way he bears up under misfortune."

Plutarch

Booker T. Washington

"EDUCATOR"

...was the founder of the Tuskegee Institute. He urged African Americans to uplift themselves through education and financial advancement.

1856–1915

Booker T. Washington was ten years old when he went to work in a salt furnace and coal mine. He lived in the South through the Civil War and endured a life similar to most people of his race: at that time, abject poverty and second-class status. What most of us would have looked upon as a plague of adversity, Washington himself looked upon it as a tilled garden for the growth of his own personal strength and the perfection of his focus and perspective.

Booker T. Washington was a self-made man who overcame the prejudices of his day, without bitterness, to become an educated, successful man. He met with great personal sacrifice, but took his own miserable circumstances and found a way to make his life a pleasurable and rewarding one. He became a teacher to other determined black students. Washington went on to become the organizer and principal of what is now Tuskegee University in Alabama. He made this institution into a major center for industrial and agricultural training and, in the process, became a well-known public speaker.

BOOKER T. WASHINGTON

Mr. Andy Andrews
P.O. Box 2761
Gulf Shores, Alabama 36547

Dear Andy,

You pose a very serious question about my life. I have never cared for what the world calls fame. My life has never been free of problems, and I am proud to say that I have used my setbacks as instruments of learning and teaching. I do want you and your readers to know that I never became discouraged over anything that I set out to accomplish. I have begun everything in my life with the idea that I could succeed; and this is the most sound advice I can give anyone.

I was born in 1856 on a plantation, the son of a slave; but to everyone's surprise, that was not my obstacle. My life had its beginnings in the midst of the most miserable, desolate, and discouraging surroundings. For as long as I can remember, my life has always been occupied with some form of labor. But, I recall that I had an intense longing to learn to read. As a small child, I was determined, if nothing else, that I would get enough education to enable me to read. My mother managed to get ahold of an old copy of a Webster's "blue-back" spelling book, which contained the alphabet. Within a few weeks, I mastered a great portion of the alphabet. I hungered to go to school, but to my disappointment, my stepfather discovered I had financial value and would not spare me to go to school. That decision seemed to cloud my every ambition. Despite this disappointment, I was determined to learn something. I applied myself with greater commitment than ever to the understanding of the blue-back speller.

One day, while I was working at the coal mine, I overheard two miners talking about a school for colored people in Virginia. The opportunities were provided by which poor but worthy students could work out all or a part of the cost of board, and at the same time be taught some trade or skill. This school, The Hampton Normal and Agricultural Institute, seemed to me that it must be the greatest place on earth. I was determined to go to that school, although I had no idea where it was, or how far it was, or how I was going to reach it. All I knew was that I was on fire with one ambition, and that was to go to Hampton.

In the fall of 1872, I was determined to make an effort to go to school. No one completely sympathized with me in my ambition, and my mother thought that I was on a wild-goose chase. At any rate, I had a few dollars, and I decided I would get on my way to Hampton. On my way to Hampton, I experienced for the first time what the color of my skin meant. I reached a little hotel with hopes of begging my way into the landlord's good graces. But without even asking if I had any money, the man at the desk refused to even consider providing me with food or lodging. I felt disappointed, but my whole soul was bent upon reaching Hampton, so I did not have time to have any bitterness towards the hotel keeper. The next day, I began my journey again by walking and begging for rides. I reached the city of Richmond, which was about 82 miles from Hampton. At this point, I was tired, dirty, and hungry, and it was very late. I was completely out of money and miserable. I needed lodging but they all wanted money, and that was what I did not have. I had come too far to turn back. At this point, I was everything but discouraged. I came upon a part of the street where the board sidewalk was elevated. I crept under the sidewalk and lay for the night upon the ground, with my satchel for a pillow. The next morning, I found myself refreshed and starved. I managed to acquire a job on a large ship, unloading cargo. The captain was so pleased with my work that he told me I could continue working for a small amount per day. I worked for a few days and bought food and added the rest to pay my way to Hampton. I finally reached Hampton with exactly 50 cents with which to begin my education.

This had been a long and eventful journey, but the sight of the school building seemed to have rewarded me for all that I had undergone. The sight of the school gave me new life. Life now had a new meaning, and I resolved to let no obstacle prevent me from putting forth the highest effort to accomplish the most good in the world.

I presented myself to the head teacher for assignment to a class. I know I did not make a pleasant impression, and I could see that there were doubts in her mind about admitting me. I saw her admitting other students, and this added to my discomfort. I knew that I could do as well as or even better than, anyone, if I were just given the chance to show what was in me. After a few hours, the head teacher said to me that the adjoining room needed sweeping. At that moment it occurred to me that here was my chance. Never did I receive an order with more delight. I swept the room three times and dusted everything four times. I had the feeling that in a large degree my future depended upon the impression I made upon the teacher in the cleaning of that room. She inspected the room thoroughly and was unable to find a speck of dirt or dust. Right there and then she admitted me to the institute. I was one of the happiest souls on earth. The sweeping of that room was my college examination. The sweeping of that room paved the way for me to get through Hampton. The head teacher offered me a position as janitor. I gladly accepted it because it was a place where I could work out nearly all the cost of my board. The work was hard and demanding, but I stuck to it.

So you see, Andy, there was never a time, no matter how dark and bleak the days and nights may have been, when one plan did not always remain with me, and that was a persistence to succeed. I know I did not get as far as I did without the help of many people, and for that I am grateful. The older I become, the more I am convinced that there is no education that one can attain from books that is equal to that which can be gotten from contact with people who know what they are doing and have been in my similar position. So I leave you with this thought, "Remember that no matter how small or menial the task may be, the success in that accomplishment may pave the way to your future."

Sincerely,

Booker T. Washington

Booker T. Washington

Abraham Lincoln

"PRESIDENT"

*...sixteenth president
of the United States.
He is responsible for the abolition
of slavery.*

1809–1865

Abraham Lincoln has always been my favorite president. He is an outstanding American example of one who has taken adversity and seen it through to a grand success. The Great Emancipator, though best remembered for his shining leadership qualities as president during the Civil War, experienced a number of previous trials which helped groom him for greatness. This masterful statesman was nearly excluded from political life due to a lack of formal education, a foreboding stature, a demonstrated inability toward fiscal responsibility in his personal business, and his controversial view against slavery.

Lincoln was a gentle but determined man, who saw his objectives through with tenacity and the ability to evaluate his own shortcomings with an aim toward self-improvement. This was his key to accomplishment. At a time of crisis, when hatred overcame the bonds of brotherhood and the unity of a nation, it was the wisdom of this awkward leader that brought us together again.

ABRAHAM LINCOLN

Andy Andrews
P.O. Box 2761
Gulf Shores, Alabama 36547

Dear Andy:

I received your letter several days ago and was intrigued by your request. After spending no small amount of time considering the matter, even I must admit surprise at the number of my failures that I recall.

As you know, I dropped out of grade school. My education from that point consisted of borrowed books and newspapers. I worked odd jobs throughout my teens, mostly manual labor, until in my early twenties I had saved and borrowed enough to open a country store. This was to be my life's work. I was very proud of the store, but in only a short time it had failed, and I was broke. It took me more than fifteen years to pay off all the debts.

Meanwhile, I went back to the borrowed books. Reading and working construction consumed most of my time and energy during that period. Books on the legal system were a particular favorite, and after a few years, I actually managed to become a lawyer. This, I must tell you, came as quite a surprise to everyone who knew me. Using my lack of formal education as a basis, it seems they had decided the limits of my career. To be quite honest, their doubts only served to fuel my resolve.

The practice of law agreed with me. I enjoyed the work, and I believe my clients, too, have been satisfied. Things went so well, in fact, that after a number of years, friends and colleagues encouraged me to campaign for the House of Representatives. To make a long story short—I lost! I ran again. I lost again. I also ran for the Senate not once, but twice. I was defeated both times.

After these major rejections of my beliefs and ideas, virtually no one, friends or family, believed I had a future as a political leader. The criticisms also took on a more personal nature. I was proclaimed by the press to be "too unattractive for public office," and my manner of speaking was derided as "much too dull and slow." Confidentially, I agree with both assessments; however, in retrospect, it is a source of amusement.

Were I to give advice to you or anyone who might read our correspondence, it would be simply this: believe in yourself and persist. I am frequently perplexed when I hear someone excuse himself from life because of lack of education, no finances, or no support. Because of my own experience, I understand those feelings, but I have always believed that the difficulty of an obstacle is in direct proportion to the value of the reward. Problems have always managed to ultimately encourage me. I see them not as dead ends, but as guides in my life.

Now, some thirty years later, I can even appreciate the failure of my store. It was devastating at the time, but had it prospered, you would not have asked me to write this letter. And surely, I would not have written it from the White House.

Sincerely,

Abraham Lincoln

"The giants of the race have been made
of concentration, who have struck
sledge-hammer blows in one place
until they have accomplished
their purpose."

Orison Swett Marden

Robert Peary

"EXPLORER"

...discovered the North Pole. Peary also discovered and named Independence Bay on the northeast coast of Greenland.

1856–1920

In his letter, Robert Peary explains that most people never find gold because they are unwilling to examine the dirt. It is the attitude of those people willing to dig through the dirt, to subject themselves to unpopular and uneasy tasks, that compel them to press on until great achievements have been realized. Robert Peary was an adventurer. He was in the American navy and noted as a civil engineer. His spirit urged him to venture beyond the known limitations of the world and to discover what else was out there. Much of his life was spent in the frozen wastelands of the world on a quest for discovery.

Peary was instrumental in the discovery and understanding of Inuit (Eskimo) life. He proved that Greenland was an island and not a continent. Robert Peary was accustomed to physical discomfort—the normal atmosphere of his customarily frozen surroundings. It was the emotional discomfort, born of a jeering society, which posed his biggest challenge. That was all set aside after Peary refused to be shackled by the attitudes of others and became the first man to reach the forbidding North Pole.

ROBERT PEARY

Mr. Andy Andrews
P.O. Box 2761
Gulf Shores, Alabama 36547

Dear Sir,

The storms in my life began almost as soon as my life began. My father died of pneumonia when I was but two years of age. I was raised by an adoring mother who treated and even dressed me sometimes like a girl. It was not an uncommon occasion when I had to fight another boy whose laughter had grown too loud.

My mother moved around quite a bit and transferred me almost twice yearly to different schools. Since "picking at the new kid" is considered sport by most children, I was in for a rough time. Soon, however, I learned to ignore the taunts and catcalls I received, and slowly they died down. This was a valuable lesson I remembered as an adult.

I still generally regard the first fifty-two years of my life as being composed of one failure after another. As an explorer, every adventure I undertook was open to ridicule. According to the news media, my friends, and even my extended family, the expeditions I began were ridiculous. The goal I had set for myself, everyone said, was too high. "Doomed to Fail" was the caption under my picture in the newspaper as my men and I set sail on another attempt at our objective.

And fail we did. On that particular expedition, I broke my leg in a shipboard accident before we even landed. On another, most of my toes had to be amputated after my feet became frozen, but I was up and working again as soon as I could. Each time, we returned to jeers and a sarcastic public. Over and over again, I heard that I was attempting the impossible.

Challenges are worth many times their weight in gold. Most people never see the gold because they don't examine the dirt. They are so busy trying to get away from the challenge or forget the challenge that they never discover its true value.

From my childhood, I learned to ignore the taunts of ignorant people. Rather than attempt something great themselves, they will ridicule the efforts of others.

From my failed expeditions, I learned new styles of navigation, proper techniques of dressing and eating to deal with severe cold, and the power of a positive mental attitude.

On April 6, 1909, all the hard lessons and physical toughness I had gained came together. I became the first man to reach the North Pole. Fame and prosperity followed, of course, but I've often commented that none of it would have been possible without the storms. And most certainly, the earlier disdain of family and friends made victory that much sweeter!

Sincerely,

Admiral Robert E. Peary

"An obvious fact about negative feelings
is often overlooked. They are caused by us,
not by exterior happenings. An outside
event presents the challenge,
but we react to it.
So we must attend to the way we take things,
not to the things themselves."

Vernon Howard

Jim Thorpe

"ATHLETE"

...in 1912 he was recognized as the worlds' greatest all-around athlete.

1888–1953

Jim Thorpe, who was of Indian and Irish descent, is most famous for his exploits on the gridiron, although he excelled at numerous sports. He is regarded by many as the greatest all-around athlete in history. His victories in the decathlon and the pentathlon in the 1912 Olympic Games marked the first time any track-and-field participant had won both grueling events. Thorpe played major league baseball from 1913 to 1919 and professional football from 1915 to 1929. Although he was stripped of his Olympic medals in 1913 for having accepted money in a semiprofessional baseball league—a common practice for many amateurs of the day—he was later exonerated and his records reinstated.

—————— JIM THORPE ——————

Mr. Andy Andrews
P.O. Box 2761
Gulf Shores, Alabama 36547

Dear Andy,

I was born in a one-room cabin made of cotton-wood and hickory, south of the town of Bellemont, in the plains country of the Oklahoma Territory. Nine-and-a-half pounds at birth, I was a member of the Sac and Fox tribe. My mother called me Wa-tho-huck, which means "Bright Path," but to the world, I became known as Jim Thorpe.

Most people don't know that I was born a twin. Charlie and I didn't look very much alike. His hair was brown while mine is black, and his complexion was darker. He was, however, my best friend and constant companion. We did everything together. We learned to hunt and fish, set traps for quail and rabbit—Charlie was a part of me. Then Charlie was gone.

Nothing has hurt me as much before or since. Charlie and I were excited about a hunting trip our father was to take us on, when Charlie became ill. It only seemed to be a cold, but Mom insisted he stay home. My father and I were away for two days. I got my first deer the second morning and was so anxious to tell my brother about it that my father agreed to leave immediately. When we got home, Charlie was dead.

For a time after that, I felt as though I were the one who had died. I couldn't sleep and didn't want to eat. I ran. Mostly, I ran with tears in my eyes, but I ran. I ran every morning, every day after school, and at night while my family slept.

I guess for a time I was running from my grief, but one day I began running toward something instead of away. I was always a better athlete than Charlie—bigger lungs maybe. One day we were playing follow the leader and Charlie just couldn't go any farther. He plopped down on the ground. I turned to stop and he motioned me on. "Don't quit," he said. "Run for me."

Turns out, that's what I did. For the rest of my life I ran for my brother. Sure, it was tough to lose him, but his memory, his sense of humor, and an offhand comment during a childhood game had profound impact on my life. All that running turned me into what some people called the greatest athlete in history.

It is a terrific lesson, isn't it? Never give up. Keep running to your future—to your hopes and dreams. I suppose I'll leave you with that specific message. Consider this a gift from Charlie to me to you.

When you experience a tragedy or a downturn in your life, just remember that Jim Thorpe believes in you. So don't quit. Run for me.

Your friend,

Jim Thorpe

Jim Thorpe

"You must begin to think of yourself
as becoming the person you want to be."

David Viscott

George Washington

"PRESIDENT/ STATESMAN"

*...was commander in chief of the
Continental Army during the
American Revolution. Later, he
became the first president
of the United States.*

1732–1799

It has been nearly 200 years since George Washington walked among the throngs of admiring patriots of early America. His legacy has not diminished, and his legend is set into the very foundation of our country. Washington never wanted to be president. It was a point of conflict for him, as he treasured his own personal life with his wife, Martha. It was because of Washington's willingness to sacrifice his own desires to help lay hold of the American dream that he secured this dream for generations to come. American leaders of our day might do well to stop and consider what George Washington would do if he were in their shoes today.

Washington was first and foremost a warrior. Incredibly bold in the face of fire, he inspired his countrymen to follow an example of bravery and determination. His leadership capabilities, wisdom, and character were forged within the killing range of enemy cannons and muskets. It is ironic that many of his abilities as a leader were tested and formed in the frozen conditions of Valley Forge. Washington faced many storms of perfection in his life. He is an example of hope and the reality that such storms are often what we need to fuel the run to success.

GEORGE WASHINGTON

Mr. Andy Andrews
P.O. Box 2761
Gulf Shores, Alabama 36547

My Dear Mr. Andrews,

Of all the names and honors bestowed upon me throughout the ages, the one that I have found the most amusing is "father of our country." I must admit to you, Mr. Andrews, that as a "father" I made many, many mistakes. Far too numerous to mention the occasions when this infant collection of former colonies, now called states, was posed to collapse upon itself. Taxes, a unified system of government, even whiskey were issues upon which adult representatives, even the states they represented, came to blows.

However, the mistakes made in my latter years bore little resemblance to the grave blunders suffered during the dawn of my military career. These "lessons" cost the lives of many brave and honorable men under my command and nearly resulted in my demise as well. As luck and the providence of the Almighty would have it, I was able to learn from my misfortunes and turn defeat into glorious victory.

In 1754, I was a young major in the Virginia militia. I was ordered to lead a force of three hundred and fifty raw recruits through the wilderness to French-occupied Fort Duquesne at the present-day site of Pittsburgh, Pennsylvania. Moving forward at the rate of four miles per day, we arrived at a spot some forty miles from Fort Duquesne. Here we erected our own fort, named Necessity. By the standards of Fort Duquesne, it was a sad comparison, but it served our purposes.

We continued our advances toward the enemy, who in turn found it more advantageous to advance upon us. Seven hundred French soldiers and their Indian allies fell upon us. In short order they drove us back into Fort Necessity. It was there we learned our fort would never live up to its name. Its location made it impossible to defend. It was surrounded by hills from which our French and Indian attackers could fire down upon us. The enemy took its time, firing endlessly from behind rocks and trees. Many of my men were drunk on rum, and our casualties began to mount. We soon totaled thirty dead and seventy wounded; many more deserted. In nine short hours it was over. I was forced to give over my sword and sign hastily drafted articles of surrender by candle in a driving rainstorm. I had lost my first battle, my first fort, and my first command. Because of my humiliating defeat, the French now controlled the entire Ohio valley, and Indians now freely attacked settlers all along the frontier.

However, as I limped home to Virginia and my beloved Mount Vernon, I resolved to learn from this failure. I later was able to use the guerrilla warfare of the Indians. My frontiersmen would learn from my mistakes at the Battles of Trenton and Kings Mountain. They would sneak in and attack the proud British forces from the cover of rocks and trees, thus routing them and humiliating them on their way to ultimate victory for our new nation in the Revolutionary War.

Mr. Andrews, from these early disasters, I learned that failure is not fatal, although it almost was in my case. More important, failure can be a classroom from whence the most profound lessons can be gleaned. This, above all, is the testament of my life and career. I only hope it serves your readers well.

Yours truly,

George Washington

"The world is so constructed,
that if you wish to enjoy its pleasures,
you must also endure its pains.
Whether you like it or not,
you cannot have one without the other."

Swami Brahmananda

Charles A. Lindbergh

"AVIATOR"

…was a Pulitzer Prize winner. He became the first person to make a nonstop solo flight across the Atlantic Ocean.

1902–1974

Charles A. Lindbergh, American aviator, was the first person to fly solo, non-stop, across the Atlantic. Acclaimed a hero both in Europe and the U.S., he was commissioned a colonel in the U.S. Air Service Reserve and became a technical advisor to commercial airlines. He traveled worldwide, making goodwill tours on behalf of the U.S.

During the peak of his fame, a terrible tragedy interrupted Lindbergh's life. His first child, 19-month-old Charles, Jr., was kidnapped and murdered. The fierce publicity resulting from this case caused Charles and his wife, Anne, to flee America and settle in Europe.

Because Lindbergh admired the German air force and felt that the U.S. should stay out of World War II, public opinion turned against him, and he lost his commissions. In time, however, he recovered the public's acceptance and continues to be a revered figure today. In addition to his expertise in flying, he wrote several well-received books, including his autobiography, *We, and The Spirit of St. Louis*, for which he was awarded the Pulitzer Prize. It is interesting to note that "Lucky Lindy" wasn't always so lucky, and when he was successful, luck had nothing to do with it.

CHARLES LINDBERGH

Mr. Andy Andrews
P.O. Box 2761
Gulf Shores, Alabama 36547

Dear Andy,

Without meaning to be facetious, I can clearly claim to have experienced more extreme ups and downs than most people. I guess you already know that I achieved worldwide fame when I was only twenty-five, being the first person ever to fly nonstop transatlantic, from New York City to Paris—in a plane named *The Spirit of St. Louis.*

As a result, I was acclaimed an international hero overnight. Many offers came my way, and I was soon well off financially. I had a lovely wife, the former Anne Morrow, daughter of an American diplomat, and we soon had a beautiful baby boy.

But it's almost as if too much happiness isn't meant to last. Our infant son was cruelly kidnapped and murdered, and my life went into a tailspin. I didn't know if I could ever recover from it.

Not only was there the pain of the awful incident, but the nation-wide publicity resulting from it, which became unbearable to me. Reporters and the public besieged my wife and me at every turn. Once a happy, carefree young man, I now became saddened and bitter.

But I knew I had to come to grips with this tragedy. I had to overcome it. The best plan seemed to be to live elsewhere, at least for a while. So we went abroad and settled in Europe. Naturally, I kept busy in my own profession.

I toured the continent, studying the air forces of various countries, and came to the conclusion that the German air force was superior to that of any country in Europe. I even accepted a decoration from Adolf Hitler.

Sadly, as the world was on the verge of plunging into the Second World War, many of my American compatriots came to view me as a traitor to the U.S. How can I explain that this was not the case? I simply spoke the truth as I saw it.

Many of my statements were misunderstood, and this caused me great pain. Not only did I respect the German air force, but also stated that the Nazis could form a buffer against Communism. At that time in our history, Communism was viewed as a terrible evil, and I wanted more than anything for that creed to be prevented from entering American shores.

I also felt that America should stay out of the war. Is there anything wrong in being opposed to war? I wanted to protect our boys from being slaughtered.

Be that as it may, I was made to suffer again. Since I was criticized for being pro-German, I was forced to resign my commission in the U.S. Air Corps and my membership in the National Advisory Committee for Aeronautics.

Again, life seemed unbearable.

But time, as well as fortitude, heals all wounds. Public opinion softened. By the time World War II broke out, I was asked to become a consultant to aircraft manufacturers and was again sent on missions on behalf of the U.S. Air Force, both to Europe and the Pacific.

I mention this last point with particular purpose. On one such mission to the Pacific, I saw and fell in love with the beautiful island of Maui, Hawaii. There we built a house—by then my wife and I had five beautiful children. And there I chose to spend my retirement years.

Looking back on my life, I can truly say that I encountered many storms of great severity. And each time, it seemed that I could not continue. But each time, I took my courage in hand, and persevered.

I always followed my dream—high, high into the sky and beyond.

Andy, thank you for this opportunity to share my thoughts and feelings with you.

Sincerely,

Charles A. Lindbergh

J. Paul Getty

"FINANCIER"

*...became an independent
oil producer in 1914. From WW II
until his death, he remained one
of the richest men in the world.*

1892–1976

    J. Paul Getty was one of the great American oil barons. He and a handful of others such as John D. Rockefeller changed that sticky crude from a nuisance into "black gold." Their toughness and riverboat gambler mentalities transformed our country from an agricultural nation to an industrialized superpower. And Getty was destined to become the greatest gambler of them all.

    He grew up as a child of wealth. Like many in his situation, he seemed to be well on his way to living the life of the idle rich. Instead, he learned to start over. He learned to scratch and fight and risk. He learned how to be a winner. And he did not stop learning . . . and winning . . . until he reached his goal of being the best. He wasn't perfect—none of us are—but he presents us with a tremendous lesson in storm survival. And that's why his letter is here.

J . P A U L   G E T T Y

Mr. Andy Andrews
P.O. Box 2761
Gulf Shores, Alabama 36547

Dear Mr. Andrews,

I am often asked, "How did you become the world's richest man?" I am asked this question as though there were some simple mathematical formula for achieving success. While I'm never ashamed of the title, let me make it clear that such was never my ambition. Having money for money's sake alone is rarely satisfying. I learned this myself as a young man. My father was an insurance salesman whose life was forever changed when he saw the oil fields of western Pennsylvania. My mild-mannered, precise, Christian Scientist father made a surprisingly good oilman, and we grew quite wealthy by the time I entered college.

At that time, I wanted little to do with business. Wine, women, and song were the order of the day. I toured Europe and saw the beginnings of the First World War. All I cared about was sowing my wild oats and enjoying the benefits of my father's wealth. Once, I married twice within a year. I was young and rich . . . and bored.

Out of desperation, I reluctantly entered "my father's business." And fell in love. It was then that I discovered my life's goal: to become the biggest and most successful oilman in the business. Now, keep in mind that the oil fields of Oklahoma, where I started, were under frontier conditions. Men still carried sidearms into primitive hotels. Food was served in shacks down mud roads. My competitors were even rougher still, cutthroat men who were almost outlaws. I had nowhere near the money they had. My father and I had fallen out; he sent me only a pittance with which to buy oil leases, and even less to live on. This created a feud between father and son which lasted until his death and nearly brought about my downfall.

To overcome these obstacles, I learned several important lessons:

Look for the weak link. I had found some land which looked promising early in my career but realized I could not match my competitors' ability to buy it. My solution was to pay a banker to whom my competitors owed money to bid for me, knowing full well my enemies would never bid against their creditor. The result was a buy for me with huge profits.

When blocked, look for an alternate route. My small oil company could produce oil, but needed oil refineries and pipelines to really compete with Standard Oil and other giants. I could never afford these on my own. My solution was to buy stock in refinery and pipeline companies until I had a controlling interest. The result was that I achieved my goal and saved millions.

Finally, don't give up on your risks. I was in the midst of buying stock in this manner when I faced my greatest storm. My father died and left the vast bulk of his estate to my mother. I was left only $500,000, and half of this had to be paid back to my father's estate for debt I previously owed. Worse yet, control of Getty Oil Company was left to the lawyers who executed my father's will. And then, the Great Depression started. Men such as George Eastman, who had fortunes much greater than mine, killed themselves rather than face their losses. When oil prices plummeted, the stock I did have became virtually worthless. I, too, pondered my imminent collapse. I considered retirement with what little money I had left. I was convinced I would be just another footnote to this economic disaster. Getty Oil Company would be but a memory. But then, I hit on an idea. Since stock prices were low, I would buy, instead of sell like everyone else. My own mother, and many others, said I was crazy. But I continued acquiring stock and stretching myself thinner and thinner. When World War II erupted, oil prices climbed, and my risky maneuver made me millions in profits. The investors who had bailed out now had nothing.

Remember, Mr. Andrews, that the true leader is the one who keeps his head in the midst of the storm. Perseverance is more often the key to success than all the wisdom of Solomon. Combine that tenacity with some intestinal fortitude, and you, too, will win.

Yours Truly,

J Paul Getty

J. Paul Getty

"Talk back to your internal critic.
Train yourself to recognize and write down
critical thoughts as they go through your mind.
Learn why these thoughts are untrue and
practice talking and writing back to them."

Robert J. McKain

Marie Curie

"PHYSICIST"

...was the first woman to win the Nobel Prize. Curie coined the term "radioactive" to describe her early experiments with uranium.

1867–1934

Madame Marie Curie is usually thought of as a Frenchwoman. She was not. She was Polish, and had come to France in order to seek a formal education that she was denied in her homeland because of her gender. She is remembered as one of the greatest scientists and physicists in modern history. She was a Nobel Prize laureate who, in partnership with her French husband and physicist Pierre Curie, discovered the elements polonium and radium.

Ironically, Marie was an antifeminist. She had too many important tasks at hand to be bothered with feminism, an ideal which she considered tiresome and pointless. In spite of Marie Curie's refusal to associate or speak for their platforms, she was hailed by feminists as one of their idols. Madame Curie's work and dedication transcended such boundaries and won the approval of fellow scientists worldwide.

The dangers of working with such powerfully radioactive materials as uranium, polonium, and radium were unknown to anyone at that time. Plagued with what we now know to be radiation sickness, Marie Curie was continually in poor health. Nevertheless, she proceeded undaunted with her work until she finally died as a result of fatal doses of these radioactive elements. Fifty years after her death, her wooden laboratory chair, in which she sat to record her experimental findings in scientific ledgers, still contained such dangerously high levels of radioactivity that it was not safe to approach. Yet, her tireless scientific work, which took her own life, has led to many methods of healing through radioactive means.

Marie Curie

Mr. Andy Andrews
P.O. Box 2761
Gulf Shores, Alabama 36547

Dear Mr. Andrews,

I have been remembered as a heroine of science, though it was not my intent to be such. I simply had an unquenchable desire for scientific discovery. In light of my successes, I have a rather lengthy tale of hardship. How easily are such afflictions overlooked and forgotten in the radiance of sweet victory and success. Ah, but herein lies my task of which you have requested. I shall recall the loss, the heartbreak, and the trial which helped to shape my ultimate destiny. Surely, without them, I could not have found the road to discovery and fulfillment.

At the end of a darkened cobbled street, leading from the red-brick battlements of the city walls of Warsaw, Poland, I began my childhood. I was named Maria Sklodowska. Poland was under the boot of the Russian army in the most ruthless period of the Russianization of my country. Hunger, death, and poverty were close acquaintances of the village folk among whom I lived. My father taught physics and instilled in me a great desire for learning. I learned much and quickly, as poverty had forced my family to live in the schoolhouse where my parents taught. But as I grew into my teenage years, I discovered that any secondary education for me would be out of the question while under the Russian-dominated system. I was a woman, and the Russians would not approve of it.

With my nationality and gender both withholding the promise of an education and advancement, I joined an underground educational society of like-minded women. It could have meant a violent and immediate death at the hands of the Russians should we be discovered. Nevertheless, I gained much knowledge during these years of meeting in basements and other such hiding places. I watched my mother and sister die during this time, fallen to diseases associated with poverty and malnourishment. There were times I broke under the strain. I suffered a nervous breakdown and had to be sent away from home to recuperate for the better part of a year. My tears are threatening even now at these memories. My heart hardened, and I swore that nothing would ever stop me from accomplishing what I set my mind to doing. I took on an introspective nature, and a total refusal to compromise. I was resolved to leave Poland.

I believed that the greatest rewards in life were those to be worked for with the mind. I made my way—with great difficulty—to France in order to attend school, and I worked any number of menial jobs to finance my education. The sacrifices are too numerous to account for here. I met my husband, Pierre Curie, while in college. My love for him was matched only by my own desire to seek out my destiny as a physicist. We were married and worked closely with one another in the area of science. And so, I became Marie Curie. I reached an incredible milestone when I graduated with my four-year degree in physics. But soon I had another concern: I was going to be a mother.

I had to employ a servant to care for my child if I was to continue with my career, and this brought the guilt and difficulties of a working mother. Even in your age, the problems facing a working mother are formidable. My age was not so tolerant of such a decision. There were few enough women laboratory physicists who had continued their careers after graduation, but for a young mother to be involved in this way only weeks after giving birth—even in the more liberal atmosphere of France— was looked on as extraordinary, if not neglectful. Nevertheless, I remained single minded about my scientific future.

After earning a four-year degree, I determined to obtain my doctorate in physics. For a woman, the precedents for this were almost nonexistent, even outside France, but I expected no concessions. By this time, I had developed great self-confidence and self-sufficiency out of necessity. I never embraced any feminist cause and saw full well that I could only achieve equality by making for myself the conditions under which I could compete with men on equal terms. I approached this next stage of my career with absolute refusal to tolerate any thought of deflection. Taking on such a venture so soon after having a baby was perhaps fueled by my own perverse streak, which was stimulated by the challenge of adversity.

X rays had just been discovered, and nearly everyone in the scientific community had chosen to pursue its amazing discovery with further experimentation. I avoided this obvious avenue, however, and opted to investigate the properties of uranium and its puzzling nature of darkening photographic plates through the plate's protective coverings. This property I would later name "radiation." This was virgin scientific territory. My investigation of uranium led me to consider the same radiation properties in other organic materials.

I had to begin everything from scratch. I needed a laboratory. I needed utensils and experimental equipment. I needed large amounts of uranium and other compounds which I had determined to study. I also, of course, needed financing, as I had not only my research to fund, but a family as well. At first, I begged and persuaded what sympathetic colleagues I could find. I was able to obtain the bare minimum of paraphernalia and working space in order to conduct my experiments. I used tools so primitive that a twentieth-century schoolboy in a chemistry lab would now find them laughable. But the scheme worked!

My experiments met with early phenomenal success. I discovered new properties of known elements and published my findings. My husband left his work with the properties of gravitation in order to assist me in my staggering new discoveries. Our efforts were rewarded yet again when I discovered an entirely new element. It was a radioactive element I named "polonium," after my beloved homeland, Poland. Many scientists found it difficult to believe that a woman could be capable of the original work in which I was involved. My discoveries were challenged and argued aggressively by the scientific societies, but found to be accurate nevertheless. Pierre would only amplify my praises all the more, refusing to take any credit which was born of my scientific work.

My adversities continued, as did my triumphs. I continued my labor in near freezing, leaky shacks that substituted for scientific laboratories. I gave myself over to manual labor, crushing rocks by the literal tons with a metal bar to glean, by numerous additional chemical processes, the precious few ounces of the pure radioactive material I sought. The work was utterly exhausting. Illness continually troubled me. But I was rewarded yet again by finding another element previously unknown to mankind. It was hundreds of times more radioactive than my first discovered element, polonium. It indeed was more than a thousand times more radioactive than uranium. I called it "radium." This was to be the jewel in my crown of scientific achievement.

In 1906, eleven years after our marriage, my beloved Pierre was killed in a freak collision with a horse-drawn carriage. I almost gave everything up after that. I was so completely devastated that I had no desire or willingness to continue for a time. Indeed, I had no money to continue even had I desired to. But eventually I realized my calling and remembered that Pierre had always so desired my scientific attainment to reach its full potential. So, I persisted again. The great American, Andrew Carnegie, recognized my scientific contributions to mankind and endowed $50,000 to the "Curie Scholarships" for the continuation of my studies.

My experiments and discoveries had changed the world of science. Although I endured terrible adversity, I held an almost ridiculous optimism. I now look back upon that old experimental shack and realize that it not only held the worst and hardest times of my life, but also held the most wonderful times of my life. Yours truly,

Marie Curie

Christopher Columbus

"EXPLORER"

*...achieved fame by
discovering what is now known
as America.*

1451–1506

When Christopher Columbus stepped ashore in the Americas in October of 1492, the scale of his discovery was more extraordinary than even he could imagine; two great continents with a land mass larger than the world he knew. Few events have altered the course of history as drastically as that fateful landfall. From virtually the moment Columbus planted the flag of Spain in the sand of a small Caribbean island, both he and his achievements have been thrust into the realm of history, mythology, and legend.

This is the man who discovered the new world, and the visionary who was driven to make that first epic voyage across the "green sea of darkness." Born in Genoa, Italy, as the son of a weaver, he began to carry on a legacy in his father's trade. Christopher, however, was born to a much higher calling. Genoa was home to a very large sea port. Columbus abandoned the weaver's trade and sought a life at sea. This early seafaring experience, enhanced by his inquisitive and scientific nature, precipitated his ambition to seek out the very limits of the farthest western horizon.

CHRISTOPHER COLUMBUS

Mr. Andy Andrews
P.O. Box 2761
Gulf Shores, Alabama 36547

Dear Sir,

I will here again reflect upon the celebrated achievements of my life. The sweetness of these memories has been strongly seasoned with irony, as I consider that my historic discoveries came about certainly as much "in spite of me" as they did "because of me." My experiences have validated to me that diligent toil in pursuit of one's dreams and following the convictions of one's heart beyond all obstacles will bear the fruit of great accomplishments. I now refer to my personal diaries, which I faithfully kept from an early age. I vividly recall the path I trod toward the destiny I carved out for myself.

March 12th , 1473
For the past two years I have exerted myself toward the understanding of astronomy and its relationship to our own world. It has been a frustrating venture. Printed research and objective records relating to this subject are difficult to obtain. Accurate maps of the known world are even more rare. Some notable Greek scholars postulated that our world is a sphere. They stated they could support their theories with mathematical data. Such thinking has generally been discarded as absurd and has proven a dangerous belief, as it is blasphemous toward the teaching of the Church. I know of one such scholar who was tied to a stake in preparation to be burned alive for holding such beliefs. He sensibly recanted his conviction and was spared the flames. Still, I wonder if this could truly be so. Dare I even consider it possible? I feel a longing for the sea, as if perhaps the key to great mysteries can be found beyond its watery borders. Still, I would risk my very life if I were so bold as to hold that such an outrageous premise

were true. For a man of 22 years, it is a fearful predicament. I yearn for the truth, yet I risk my life and reputation in my quest for its discovery. Every reasonable person knows the world is flat.

September 16th, 1481

Ten years of labor! Ten years of toiling over charts, documents, and maps. Ten long years of querying the most skilled and experienced sailors of the day. There is no point in attempting to deny the conviction of my heart any longer, this certainly born of years of relentless research and assimilation of every conceivable piece of information. The world is a sphere! The world is not flat! I am made a fool in the eyes of society for my conclusion. I have become a public spectacle, the brunt of ridicule, scorn, and humiliation. Yet there is nothing that can dissuade me from this conviction. Moreover, I am certain also that I can discover a new, swifter trade route to the Indies by sailing west. One would not fall over some imaginary edge of the world, but rather sail around the earth upon the smooth surface of a sphere. I know I could prove this. I need only a financial sponsor to fund my expedition. I need 12 ships, 350 men, and supplies for the journey. I need a financier!

May 28th, 1484

I have expended much energy and redeemed all my favors among men to gain the audience of Portugal's King John II. I felt assuredly that King John was a man of understanding and wisdom. Surely, he would grasp my theories and the lucrative possibilities afforded by sponsoring this seafaring expedition. I recently petitioned him to finance a crossing of the Western Sea and have now received his response. Wretched failure! Will no one listen?! Who is this Royal Maritime Commission, who so proudly mocks my life's work?! Fools! They wallow in their own folly by depicting me as the madman! Whom can I find who will listen to reason? I need 10 well-supplied ships, maybe 200 men. I will find a financier! I will not be defeated!

January 3rd, 1487

My reputation is soiled. For years now, I have endured the agony of public humiliation for my convictions. Yet again my petition to secure financing of a westward voyage is rejected. This time words of mockery are spewed from the laughing courts of Spain and their Royal Commissions. Perhaps there is no point in further pursuing this dream. This quest is perhaps only a foolish fancy, an exercise in futility.

April 26th, 1492

Oh, wonderful day! Persistence holds magnificent rewards! King Ferdinand and Queen Isabella have finally given ear to me. They have agreed to underwrite my expedition! I set sail in four months. Three ships, 90 men. Indeed, far less than what I had first hoped for, but hope itself now seems to hold so much more promise!

August 3rd, 1492

We set sail! I can taste the tangy, salt-filled air as I breathe deeply the mist over the vast Western Sea. A strong wind is at our backs, driving our tiny fleet swiftly across the expanse of the roiling, deep-blue water. Aboard these ships, with boards and ropes creaking and straining, we journey onward in anticipation of a new world and the adventures born of new discoveries. I can hear the cry of the gulls and the cheers of the crew. I can feel the great sense of exhilaration as we depart from the harbor! I close my eyes and imagine our approach to the horizon, presenting picturesque towers of uncharted coastline cliffs.

September 28th, 1492

Nearly two full months on a westward course. No sign of land. No hints upon the horizon. Our sails hang limp on another cursed, windless summer day. Rations are desperately low. The morale of the sailors is no higher. I have been forced to record two journey ledgers. Only I possess the legitimate ledger. The other, in which I have falsely documented our traveled distance, I allow my officers to examine. I know we are now beyond the point of no return. There are not enough rations to sustain the crew if we attempt to return to Spain. Our quest now is to discover new, uncharted land—or die.

October 12th, 1492

Land! More beautiful than any upon which my eyes have ever gazed! Glorious land claimed by Cristobal Colon in the name of the King and Queen of Spain!

Alas, Sir Andrews, as history has revealed, my calculations were incorrect. I never found the elusive trade route to the Indies or Asia by sailing west. I believed the earth to be 25 percent smaller than its actual size and covered predominantly by land. Nevertheless, as is now widely known, my quest was immensely successful in the opening of the western world and in the discovery of many lands previously unknown to the European world. I embarked upon several subsequent voyages, which were much easier to arrange. They resulted in conquest and, ultimately, the establishment of trade with the New World. I gained prominence, wealth, and a historic reputation.

I remain fully persuaded that it was not so much my maritime skills, scientific ability, or clever design to embark upon such journeys at sea which are laudable, but rather my brute determination and persistence to lay hold of my dreams. Such attributes as these are the foundation of any great deed.

Yours Truly,

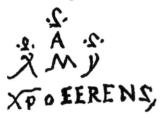

Christopher Columbus

"Win hearts, and you have
hands and purses."

Lord Burleigh

John Wayne
"ACTOR"

*...best known as a film actor
for his portrayal of rugged, honest
American heroes.* The Alamo, The
Green Berets, *and* True Grit *are some
of his most famous films.*

1907–1979

He was the Duke. He was the epitome of American manhood. He had true grit, faithfulness, and was a flag-waving patriot. Yes, John Wayne was more than just an actor. John Wayne is a legend. For years, and in more that 250 movies, he was the daring bare-fisted cowboy, the brave lawman, the war hero, the compassionate comrade, and the worthy, devoted husband. But John Wayne was more than just a man acting as someone with such admirable qualities. He is described by those who knew him best as being able to portray these attributes on screen because he was genuinely such a man.

Because of John Wayne's outspoken patriotism and his producing of such honorable films of the United States military (such as *The Green Berets*), he was awarded the Medal of Honor, the highest decoration of the U.S. military. His acting career was one of the most phenomenal in history. He had true acting ability, but because of his real character, his roles as the rugged, honest American man were riveting and seamless.

JOHN WAYNE
BATJAC PRODUCTIONS

Mr. Andy Andrews
P.O. Box 2761
Gulf Shores, Alabama 36547

Dear Andy,

Well, my parents named me Marion—that should be enough of a storm for you. Marion Michael Morrison was my given name. I was born and raised in Winterset, Iowa, where my dad worked as a pharmacist. As a child, I owned an Airedale named Duke—how I ended up with the dog's name, I'll never know.

I grew up dreaming of the military. To me, a man in uniform was the archetypal hero, and that is how I saw myself. Through my teens, I developed a very real desire for a career in the service and settled on Annapolis as my college choice.

To make a long story short, I was turned down. Flat. Even a friend of my father's with connections at the academy couldn't help. It was a devastating time, a time I saw as the end of a lifelong ambition.

As a distant second choice, and at my parents' urging, I accepted a football scholarship to the University of Southern California. In those days, show business people hung around our practices and parties. I became pretty good buddies with Tom Mix, the cowboy star. He didn't have any game tickets, and I didn't have any money, so we worked out an equitable trade: Tom Mix got my game tickets, and I got a job as the prop man on the set of his latest picture.

One afternoon, I was giving instructions to a kid about where to put this or that, and some guy stopped and cocked his head. "Could you say that again?" he asked.

I was a little aggravated at the interruption. I put my hands on my hips and said, "Say what again?"

"Never mind," he answered. "You will do nicely." It turned out that he was a big producer of radio shows. He put me in a radio series called "The Three Sheets to the Wind." It ran for two years, and that was the beginning of it all.

I ended up in more than 250 major motion pictures, won an Academy Award, traveled all over the world, had a great life, and why? Well, for starters, because I didn't get accepted to Annapolis, that's why!

Don't complain if everything doesn't happen in sync with your plans. Don't be discouraged if you are turned down or overlooked. The alternative, even if you don't see it immediately, just might start you on the greatest adventure of your life!

Sincerely,

John Wayne

"It is a mistake to suppose
that men succeed through success;
they much more often
succeed through failures....
Precept, study, advice, and example
could never have taught them
so well as failure has done."

Samuel Smiles

Babe Ruth

"ATHLETE"

...was elected to the
Baseball Hall of Fame in 1936.
He was one of the most phenomenally
gifted and popular players in
the history of his sport.

1895–1948

The Babe Ruth saga is the sports equivalent of a Horatio Alger story—a rags to riches tale that saw him rise from the streets of Baltimore to the National Baseball Hall of Fame. The way Ruth tells it, he could have died at an early age with nothing to show for his life but a stint in what we refer today as a reform school. But because he let someone special into his life and decided to associate with this mentor and motivator, rather than hang around with lowlifes and thugs, Ruth (born George Herman Ruth) became "the Babe." He honed his natural skills and channeled his anger at his parents into the swing of a bat, and in the process, turned the New York Yankees into a dynasty.

Ruth revolutionized the game by making home runs look easy. He slugged sixty round-trippers in 1927. A perennial .340 hitter who walked a lot, stole bases, and handled his outfield chores with grace, Ruth began his major league career as a pitcher for the Boston Braves. Even in that role, Ruth excelled: In two World Series (1916 and 1918), he hurled a record twenty-nine consecutive scoreless innings. But the Babe will always be known as a slugger. Yankee Stadium became known as "The House That Ruth Built." And by the time he hung up his spikes in 1935, Ruth had amassed 714 home runs, a record that held until 1974, when Henry Aaron clouted his 715th. But Aaron would never have had a record like that to chase if young George Herman Ruth had decided not to associate with that one positive influence in his life.

BABE RUTH

Mr. Andy Andrews
P.O. Box 2761
Gulf Shores, Alabama 36547

Hey, Kid,

It's kinda strange gettin' a request for a letter that someone wants to put in a book. As ya probably already know, I ain't much for writin', let alone speakin'. Usually, all anyone wants is my John Hancock, and, you bet, I'm happy as a kid playin' hooky on a sunshiny, baseball kinda day to do that sorta thing. But a book? Now that's some kinda honor.

So ya want me to talk about a storm, eh? Well, kid, my whole darned life has been one storm after another. Kinda hard to believe, I'll bet, after all the things ya've heard about my home runs and the rest of the amazing feats of the Bambino, the Sultan of Swat, the Maharajah of Mash (boy, I'll bet I didn't spell that right, but your publisher says ya've got a swell proofreader), the Behemoth of Bust. I mean, heck, they called Yankee Stadium "The House That Ruth Built"—and not just because I slugged the first home run in the very first game played there. Ya know, it don't get much better than that.

But way back when I was a tyke, I never coulda dreamed of bein' a big-league ball player. I was fat and ugly and what they called back then "incorrigible." My nose was wider than most kids' faces, and I was always laughed at and gettin' in fights in that tough neighborhood in Baltimore. Heck, when I was five, I was already stealin' stuff from stores and throwin' rocks at delivery men. By the time I was seven, I was chewin' tobacco. They tried to change me, but my ma and pa, they didn't care a lick about me and sent me to St. Mary's Industrial School.

That's funny, ya know, kid. Your folks have ya, then they figure they don't like the way ya turned out. So they try to make more babies, but six of the next seven die before they're outa diapers. So they take it out on the bad one, the rotten apple. What's even funnier is they send ya to a school where all the other boys are just as mean as you are. A buncha delinquents. A buncha inmates in a prison for kids.

It sure didn't look good for ol' George Herman Ruth Jr., I'll tell ya that much, kid. But the good Lord musta had a soft spot for me. I sure can't tell ya why. But he brought Brother Matthias into my life at just the right time. Brother Matthias was the guy in charge of disciplining the boys at St. Mary's. Maybe it was because I was so big for my age, maybe it was a miracle. Who knows, kid? But Brother Matthias saw somethin' in me, somethin' nobody else had. He saw a kid who could cream the baseball farther than anyone, who could pitch it faster than any of the other boys. And it was because of Brother Matthias that I got my one-way ticket outa St. Mary's when I was eighteen.

The rest, as they say, is history. I went on to become the greatest home run hitter in the game—and set quite a few pitching records along the way, I might add. Sure, it was my talent that did it for me, but I can't help wondering about fate, and how it enabled me to weather this particular storm. If I hadn't been forced to go to St. Mary's. If Brother Matthias hadn't believed in me. Gosh, it's a strange world.

Now, kid, I won't go into all the other storms in detail, like when I couldn't get a job managing after I hung up my spikes, like when the fans in Chicago spat on me and my wife, Claire, as we came and went from our hotel in 1932, when we were playin' the Cubs in the World Series. That, incidentally, was the series where I hit my famous "called shot" off Charlie Root. (By the way, when folks ask me if I really was callin' that homer, if I really was pointin' to center field, tellin' the whole world where I was goin' to deposit the next pitch, I answer the same way I did in the clubhouse after the game: "Check the newspapers. It's all right there in the papers." Just between you and me, kid, maybe it was another one of those miracles.)

I'm not gonna try to tell ya, kid, that my life has been one big Fourth of July parade. I've made a lot of mistakes. I drank too much, I ate too much, I smoked too many cigars, and, well, the women, they were always there—and let me tell ya, when you're as ugly as a catcher's mitt, you're more than grateful for all the female attention you can get. But then that's what got me in trouble with my first wife, and, well, I don't wanna go into it.

There's more, kid. In fact, it's almost another miracle that your letter came when it did. I ain't been feelin' so good lately, and nobody'll level with me, but I think it's the big C, cancer. The doctors are gonna do some cuttin' in the throat area, and it just don't sound good. But that's another storm that's brewin'. And it hasn't quite hit yet. Maybe I'll send ya another letter soon, if ya wanna hear about it. OK? Thanks, kid, for lettin' me get this off my chest. And remember, whenever ya step to the plate, try to hit a homer. Ya may not get one, but at least ya've given it your best shot.

Your Pal,

Babe Ruth

Babe Ruth

P.S. Remember to touch all the bases, kid.

William Shakespeare

"PLAYWRIGHT"

*...is recognized as the
greatest of all dramatists. He is
considered the supreme poet of the
English language.*

1564–1616

William Shakespeare was one of those remarkable people who just seemed to be blessed with unending talent. Most find it difficult to believe that his father, John, had been a glovemaker. John was well respected in the community of Stratford-upon-Avon, England, but he was certainly not a particularly creative man.

His son William, however, went to London, where he became a great poet and playwright. In fact, many people consider him to be not only the world's greatest playwright in the English language, but one of the greatest of all dramatists. A list of his plays would be too long to print here. But there are thirty-eight of them. *Hamlet* and *Romeo and Juliet* are two of the best known.

Perhaps the key to Shakespeare's success, aside from inborn talent, was just plain, hard work. He was also an actor who ran his own acting company. He was always in the position of needing plays to put on. So he wrote his own. In spite of the death of his young son, and a near-fatal run-in with Queen Elizabeth, the ruler of England at the time, Shakespeare survived and kept going.

His plays are still performed not only in the English-speaking world, but have been translated and presented all over the world. They probably always will be.

Globe Theatre
Southward London

William Shakespeare

Andy Andrews
P.O. Box 2761
Gulf Shores, Alabama 36547

Dear Andy:

I trust you are not offended by my informal greeting. We are, after all, both performers. Perhaps it is not generally known that I am as much an actor as a playwright, but I have had my own acting company for many years. Indeed, that is why I have been so prolific a playwright, for I have always been in the position of having to write material for the use of my company, and thus to entertain both the nobles of Elizabethan England and what we call here the groundlings (so called, for they could not afford to pay the price for chairs in the great Globe Theatre, but simply sat on the ground in front of the raised platform—the stage).

But that is getting ahead of my story. Although I was raised in the lovely, pastoral town of Stratford-upon-Avon, I later went to London to seek my fortune with my wife, the lovely Anne Hathaway, and our twin children, the boy, Hamnet, and daughter, Judith.

Things went exceedingly well for several years. I secured the patronage of important people and was able to establish my theatre company and write easily and well. I also wrote many love sonnets and longer poems, such as *Venus and Adonis*, which were well received. Were these based on personal experience? I leave that to the reader to discern. I will offer, however: a poet thrives on his imagination.

But life, unfortunately, has its pains as well as its blessings. A major calamity occurred: my beloved son Hamnet died when he was only eleven. What recourse was there for me? I could but continue to live, and for me, a poet, living meant continuing to write. I threw myself into my work.

You know the rest, perhaps. There followed a large output of plays: comedies, such as *Twelfth Night*, *Much Ado About Nothing*, *A Midsummer Night's Dream*, *As You Like It*, to name but a few. There were also tragedies, for which I am noted. These include *Hamlet*, *King Lear*, *Othello*, and *Julius Caesar*, and, of course, those tragedies which are also love stories, such as *Romeo and Juliet* and *Antony and Cleopatra*—a total of thirty-eight plays.

My interests ranging far and wide, I also chose to deal with historical figures. Thus, I wrote *King Henry IV*, *King Henry V*, *King Henry VI*, *Richard III*, and *King Henry VIII*. Mention of these, however, brings me to a serious event in my personal life. In London at that time, rebellion was in the air. It was thought that Lord Essex would rebel against his queen, Elizabeth.

One morning a small group of Essex's men approached me at the Globe and urged me to present my play *Richard II* that very night for a friend of the Earl of Essex. To refresh your memory, in this play the king is dethroned; it would have been very easy for Queen Elizabeth to identify with Richard II and thus become exceedingly angry with me for having presented the play. I am thankful that she was not in attendance.

The queen did hear of the performance, however, and was greatly troubled. I was very much afraid that my company and I would be placed out of favor with the queen and would be in jeopardy. There was a possibility we would even be accused of complicity in the conspiracy! But, gracious queen that she was, Elizabeth forgave us, and we were absolved.

(The Earl of Essex, however, did not fare so well. Elizabeth had him beheaded just a few weeks later.)

Once I overcame that bit of intrigue, I continued to experience success and prosperity. I was able to share in the profits of my acting company, first called the Chamberlain's Men, later the King's Men, and the two theatres where we operated, the Globe and the Blackfriars.

All in all, I must count my blessings. I have managed to overcome adversity and to be remembered favorably by mankind as well. I do not mean to sound pompous, but many consider me to be the greatest of all playwrights in the English language.

Perhaps, unconsciously, I have always kept in mind a line from one of my own plays: "To thine own self be true, And it must follow as the night the day, thou can'st not then be false to any man."

With sincerest and most heartfelt good wishes,
I am your servant,

Shakespeare

William Shakespeare

Andrew Carnegie

"INDUSTRIALIST/ PHILANTHROPIST"

...during the late 1800s and early 1900s, he donated more than $350 million to charities as well as various educational and cultural institutions.

1835–1919

One of the richest men in American history, Andrew Carnegie was an industrialist and philanthropist. In 1868, at the age of 33, when he had an annual income of $50,000, Carnegie said, "Beyond this, I will spend the surplus each year for benevolent purposes." Indeed, he did so. He was an incredible altruist and a benefactor to hundreds of social establishments and charities. He gave more than $350 million to educational, cultural, and charitable institutions, while living on a fraction of his income.

Andrew Carnegie made his multimillions in the steel industry. He was extremely successful in acquiring controlling interests in large steel plants and ultimately founded the Carnegie Steel Company. Carnegie, who was a man without any formal education, is responsible for providing millions of dollars to create more than 1,700 libraries, learning institutions, and charities. He also made contributions to the arts (including the establishment of Carnegie Hall) and what is now the Court of Justice of the United Nations.

CARNEGIE STEEL COMPANY

Andrew Carnegie

Mr. Andy Andrews
P.O. Box 2761
Gulf Shores, Alabama 36547

Dear Mr. Andrews,

In my time, I was the wealthiest man who ever inhabited America. I was the epitome of the American dream come true. I was described as the ultimate business tycoon, a visionary of the steel industry, a generous financial contributor to society, a bold and fearless man who flourished by pulling upon his own bootstraps while others in business drowned in bankruptcy. I am astonished at the flattering titles and honors which are often bestowed upon men merely by virtue of their possessing more money than most. I would like to remember myself as worthy of this adulation, but I would consider it hypocritical if I were not to mention my own weaknesses and shortcomings. Indeed, I was subjected to storms, but found that after I weathered them, my character was enhanced.

If I were asked to give my greatest piece of advice for successful living, it would be this: find a worthy hero to pattern yourself after and then become a hero yourself for others. Where are our heroes today? You see, I spent my youthful years in Scotland; it was a politically turbulent nation. My family was involved in politics there, and I found that the name Carnegie was well known; in fact, in some places, we Carnegies were despised for our political beliefs. I had two heroes in my youth. The first was my father, who was a strong leader and a local political champion of the common people. The other was William Wallace, the historic Scot of the movie *Braveheart.* Everything heroic centered in him. How unaware I was as a young boy of the grave need I would have in the future of a hero's inspiration. It is a tower of strength for a person of any age to have a hero.

In 1848, I was a simple thirteen-year-old Scottish immigrant in America with no formal education. My adolescent employments in America were menial tasks: a bobbin boy, a messenger, and a secretary. Where was the promising, powerful assurance of the American dream I had hoped for? Had my family and I braved the vast expanse of the Atlantic Ocean from Scotland simply to be enslaved in such disheartening circumstances? I felt my young life draining away, consumed in the triviality of abject, spiritless ventures. I worked for several years in such capacities, barely earning enough money to sustain myself. I felt that my hopes of the promised land had been dashed. Nevertheless, no hero of mine would have yielded to dismay or the prospect of whining over such apparent governing factors. So I diligently continued on in my labors, incessantly looking for an opportunity to promote myself.

This philosophy helped me to succeed in uncovering a lucrative opportunity in the steel business. Yet this business lent itself to storms of its own. When I began the business of manufacturing steel rails for the railroad industry, chemistry in the United States was an almost unknown agent in connection with the manufacture of pig iron. Although I was uneducated, I was convinced that chemistry was the one agent, above all others, most needed in the manufacture of iron and steel. I had attained a great deal of success in business by this time, but was now forced, at a critical point, to risk my entire business on my belief that chemistry would be the boon I felt it was to this industry. All that I had hoped for and toiled to attain was in the balance. I lost sleep. I was in a great deal of anguish. Again, I looked to my heroes; they were ones who had risked all they had in what they believed in. So, in the end, I took a risk and pinned my hopes on chemistry, while my competitors refused to do so. I prevailed and amassed an inconceivable amount of wealth for my time.

In September of 1873, the American economy was in panic. I was fortunate enough not to have a problem with outstanding debts, but my debtors were unable to pay their own balances. I began to carry so enormous a financial burden that no matter how wealthy I was, my business would soon be crippled. At the same time, I suffered the disappointment of watching a trusted friend and business partner abandon me to become a competitor. My friend went bankrupt, as did many American businessmen at the time. Meanwhile, I experienced racking anxiety. I could scarcely control myself. But I kept focused upon the influence of my heroes and managed to pull through this time of trial.

In 1866, my mother and brother died. Everything I had accomplished in my life was for the benefit of my family. They were the driving force behind my will to succeed. I had no pleasure in life without them. I had not yet married, and had only my family of rearing to share in my joys of life. I was devastated, and fell into a deep state of depression. I had no motivation or will to continue in my daily existence. I myself became ill and nearly died. Once again, however, I fell back upon the thought of my father and William Wallace. I allowed my body and emotions to be mended. I recovered slowly, and the future began to occupy my thoughts. I fell in love with a wonderful woman, Miss Louise Whitfield, and she agreed to be my wife.

I realized what a powerful thing it was to have heroes to follow. I determined that I would do whatever I could to help foster the recognition of those heroes who still walked the earth. I therefore founded the Hero Fund. I put forth five million dollars to reward heroes, or to support the families of heroes who perish in the effort to serve or save their fellows, and to supplement that which employers or others contribute to the support of the families of those left destitute through accidents. True heroes think not of reward. They are inspired by—and think only of—their fellow man, never of themselves.

Through my storms of perfection, I learned patience, perseverance, and wisdom, and I also gained the strength to continue. Such storms reveal the real person, and without them, one's true potential might never become manifest. I could never have reached such success without drawing on the sturdy influence of my chosen heroes. My storms were many, but I held to my optimism, as my heroes had always done. Keep a good wit, humor, a genial nature, and an irrepressible spirit. I found that a sunny disposition is worth more than a fortune. It can be cultivated. The mind, like the body, can be moved from shade to sunshine. Let us move it then!

Sincerely,

Andrew Carnegie

Andrew Carnegie

Pocahontas

"HEROINE"

...daughter of Indian chief Powhatan.
She helped keep peace
between the Indians and
Virginia settlers.

1595–1617

Pocahontas was the youngest daughter of the Indian chief Powhatan of the Chickahominy nation. She is one of those historical characters who comes across to us eternally in some legend rather than as a person in her own right.

She was not typical of the Indian culture which shaped her. She used privileges of being the youngest and favored daughter of the chief to defy many of the customs of her tradition-bound society. Two years after she came to Jamestown, Pocahontas was baptized into the Anglican community. Only five years removed from her relatively primitive wilderness life, she won the hearts of all with her charm and manners, her speech and dress, and her glowing personality.

Pocahontas will be remembered as the Indian princess who risked her life to save Captain John Smith. But the notable aspect of her short life is that she lived only twenty-two years and was the first Indian in the New World to embrace Christianity. She also became very knowledgeable in English, arithmetic, grammar, and the Bible.

POCAHONTAS

Mr. Andy Andrews
P.O. Box 2761
Gulf Shores, Alabama 36547

Dear Andy,

Before I begin telling you about my "storm," I would like to thank you for allowing me to tell you about my life, my people, and how I became a part of the English colony. Because of your request, my story can now be told to future generations in my own words, and I can dispel the myths that many people have created about me.

First of all, my birth name is Matoaka, and to the outside world, I am known as Pocahontas, which means "playful one." I am the daughter of Powhatan, the leader of the Chickahominy Confederation, who was the Chief of Chiefs, and I became known as the "Indian Princess." I led a complicated childhood, in part because I never knew mother and partly because of my father's exalted position. The most important changes in my life took place when I reached puberty and had to abandon all my childlike ways and become a woman and a respected daughter of the leader of our nation.

I was ten years old when I first saw white men, and they considered us savages, so we did not try to make direct contact. We had already known of the white man for some one hundred years. We were initially friendly to the first Europeans we encountered, but our nation became hostile after being abused and cheated by them.

In 1607, the English established a colony at Jamestown, Virginia. They came to the New World naive, anxious, and wanting a new world they could run their own way. But the harsh winters were more difficult than the settlers had planned. They struggled for many years, they never gave up, and that was a quality I admired. We had no problems with the English, and our relations were friendly, yet cautious.

In 1611, the relations between the English and the Chickahominy remained amicable and the usual amenities were observed, but the atmosphere of friendship quickly changed. My father demanded a large number of English fire sticks, bullets, and gunpowder and said he would break off relations unless he received them. It was obvious to the English that my father wanted the weapons for the sole purpose of driving the settlers into the sea, so the demand was rejected. My father abruptly terminated the barter agreement with the colony. The threat of war was serious, and the colony immediately strengthened its defense posture. We did not go to Jamestown, and the settlers were afraid to step foot on our land, except for one man, Captain Samuel Argall.

Captain Argall came to our land and presented my father with weapons that he said may be able to stop a war. What my father did not know was that the weapons he received were useless. So Captain Argall quickly hammered out a truce. And what he did next to guarantee peace would change my life forever: He abducted me and took me to Jamestown. All the English believed this would surely cause war, but only Captain Argall knew that this act would guarantee peace. He knew that my father would not make war while his beloved daughter remained a prisoner of the settlement. At the settlement, Captain Argall was placed under arrest, and Commodore Newport, whom we regarded as a friend, went to my father to explain that the kidnapping had been plotted by one man without official cognizance and promised that I would be returned unharmed.

However, no one knew that when an unmarried woman of the Chickahominy was captured by the braves of another nation, she lost her standing and was regarded as the property of the nation that had taken her prisoner. It did not matter who I was or who my father was; they were forced to disown me. What should become of me was no longer their concern, and my father would definitely not make war on the English now.

At the moment I was abducted, a new chapter of my life began. I was sixteen years old, tragically disowned by my father and nation and freed by my captors to do as I wished in an unknown world. In effect, I was no one. I did not see my life as over; instead, I saw it as an opportunity to begin to learn and teach from my experiences. During my first year in Jamestown, I concentrated my time and attention on learning English. I studied the King James Bible incessantly and mastered words and sentences. After several years, I conquered the English language. Here I was a young woman who, a few years earlier, had been a savage by the standards of the English and the Continent. Now, I was sufficiently advanced to teach reading, grammar, writing, and arithmetic, and I was studying Greek and Latin. But the most important thing I was able to do with all my knowledge was to mediate relations with the English and the Chickahominy, which I believed avoided many wars.

There were many setbacks I had to endure. In late 1615, there were several large shiploads of immigrants coming to Jamestown. Most of the newcomers had been residents of the London slums. These men and women were belligerent and had no respect for authority or law and no kinship with those who enjoyed more comforts and privileges. They immediately resented me. They declared I was an intruder, and as a member of any Indian tribe, that I was of a lower order than any Englishman. They demanded that I be expelled from the community. At that moment, I should have given up, but I didn't. I could not give up and forget everything I had learned. Instead of quitting, I needed to win them over. I talked to them and gave them an impassioned speech about my life, my tribulations, how hard I worked to get where I am, and how to never quit or give up. I changed their attitudes and won their support.

Threat of war is very serious, but in my life, it served a different purpose. It showed me how to set goals and make dreams in a world I knew nothing about. It was very upsetting to lose my Indian family, but what I gained fulfilled my life. I learned what my life meant: I should never give up or quit, and I should use my knowledge to change attitudes no matter where I am or who I encounter. Change became a very important aspect in my life, and that is why I embrace it and accept the challenge instead of becoming afraid.

Sincerely,

Pocahontas

Wolfgang Amadeus Mozart

"COMPOSER"

...has long been considered a musical genius. He is one of the most inspired composers in Western musical tradition.

1756–1791

Although a child prodigy, composing music and playing instruments by the time he was six years old, Mozart experienced intense failure as well as great early success.

As a boy, he undertook many successful tours of Europe, mostly while still in his teens. However, after reaching his twenties, he was at an impasse. Not only were many trips abroad fruitless, but his dear mother died on one such trip. He was later neglected and rejected by many aristocrats whom he had hoped would sponsor him.

He and his family suffered abject poverty and ill health while he was composing his most glorious works. His output was phenomenal: more than 600 works, including the operas *Cosi Fan Tutte*, *The Marriage of Figaro*, *The Magic Flute*, and *Don Giovanni*; the *Jupiter Symphony* and others; and many concertos for piano, violin, and other instruments. He died at the age of thirty-five.

Mozart

Mr. Andy Andrews
P.O. Box 2761
Gulf Shores, Alabama 36547

Dear Mr. Andrews,

My life has been a constant contrast between joy and sorrow. Beginning as a child prodigy in music, I thought life would be one of ease and pleasure. After all, I was skillfully playing the harpsichord and composing music by the time I was six years old! And in my native Salzburg, I attracted the attention of royalty who at first were encouraging to me—and to my father, who, a musician himself, had trained me in music.

But on a trip to Vienna, for the purpose of impressing the Empress and hoping to gain her support, I became ill with scarlet fever, a dangerous malady in those days. So our plans had to be abandoned, and we returned to Salzburg prematurely. It was an enormous setback for our entire household, for we had had to travel a long distance, and, as you know, in those days, such travel took many weeks and was very tiring.

We later went to Italy, the promised land of music, expecting great things. At first, I had some success there, and my family and I hoped that now we could become settled and wealthy. But such was not to be. In spite of my skilled musicianship and well-written scores of sonatas and symphonies, I was not invited to play for the King at the Court of Naples. He simply was not interested.

Many such incidents followed. Great expectancy followed by greater disappointment. But I went on with my work; it was the only thing that saved me. It was as if the greater the disappointment, the more passionately I threw myself into my work.

At one time, my mother and I undertook a trip to Paris. However, not only did we meet with disappointment on the professional level, but my mother died in a damp and chilly Paris hotel room. Devastated, I had to cancel my plans and return home to Salzburg.

I later married a charming woman, Constanze, and we had beautiful children. But poverty plagued us. In spite of my creating many lovely works, including the operas Cosi Fan Tutte, The Marriage of Figaro, and The Magic Flute, to name a few, and noted concertos and symphonies, there was never enough money. Those who should have sponsored and supported me took advantage and paid me less for my work than they should have. My health and that of my family suffered.

When my beloved father died, it was a black day for me. I did not know how I could go on. Later, even though the great composer Joseph Haydn touted me, I could barely survive.

Twice, my family and I were forced to change lodgings because of my inability to pay rent. This was heartbreaking poverty. I had to borrow money, but few wanted to lend to me. In some cases, I wrote musical compositions to obtain even small amounts of money, just to get out of debt. I am sorry to say that many took advantage of me and underpaid me. My family and I were ill much of the time.

One part of me struggled against misery and humiliation. But the other part found freedom from earthly matters in my music.

Perhaps it was the very storm of much of my lifetime that actually impelled me, and led me to what many have called the perfection of my art. In any case, I can only shrug and point to what I have left behind: a large body of musical work that some say will last as long as man can listen to and be moved by music.

With heartfelt good wishes, I am yours,

Wolfgang Amadeus Mozart

Moses

"PATRIARCH"

*...led the children of Israel
into the Promised Land. He received
the Ten Commandments from
God on Mount Sinai.*

1500 B.C.

I have always found it interesting that the Lord uses ordinary people to perform extraordinary tasks. Moses is a good example of a failure by human standards. He was born under threat of death and had to be abandoned by his parents. The pharaoh's daughter found his basket floating in the Nile River and raised him as her own son. But Moses messed up a royal livelihood for himself when he murdered an Egyptian he found beating a fellow Hebrew.

Moses was clumsy in speech. He was timid and shy. He was full of self-doubt and hesitancy. He did what he could to rid himself of the responsibility placed upon him by God to represent the Hebrews before Pharaoh. But to his credit, he trusted God and consequently made a few notable marks on history as a result. He was used by God to part the Red Sea. He brought down God's tablets of stone, upon which were written the Ten Commandments, and of course, he led the Israelites to the promised land. Moses was indeed a man of failures, but because of his faithfulness to God's calling, it is his great deeds which are most remembered.

MOSES

Mr. Andy Andrews
P.O. Box 2761
Gulf Shores, Alabama 36547

Dear Andy,

I suppose you know all about my early life—the floating basket of bulrushes and the whole story. I really didn't have too many problems there for a while. I grew up as one of the privileged few after being adopted by the princess.

The storm clouds really started to gather in my life as an adult. It all began with that burning bush. Now, I had never seen a burning bush before, and I haven't seen one since, but I want you to know, it got my attention!

Then I heard the voice of God. I laughed at first because I thought it was my brother Aaron. Ever since we were little boys, he had been doing a "this is God" thing where he cupped his hands over his mouth and talked real slow. "That's great, Aaron," I said. "That was a lot louder than you usually do it. Now come on and help me put out this bush!"

It was about that time when I looked down the hill. There, down in the valley was Aaron, asleep by our tent. I looked back at the bush, which was still burning, and said, "Oh my God."

"Exactly," God said, and the conversation was off and running.

As you know, He wanted me to speak to Pharaoh about letting his people go. I wasn't too keen on this at the time because Pharaoh was never in a great mood and some-times he could be downright nasty. I made a bunch of excuses about why I wasn't such a hot choice, but God (or Jehovah as we called Him then) was having none of it. I even looked around to see if Aaron would confirm my reasons for nonparticipation, but he was still asleep.

How Aaron could sleep, I'll never know. The bush was roaring and crackling, and what with God yelling, "Let my people go!" every few minutes, it was really something!

After telling God I'd give it a shot—I went to Pharaoh. Long story short, he said, "Fat chance." No big surprise there. I'd dealt with him before. The next thing that happened, though, was a surprise. The river turned to blood.

No kidding; it was real blood. At first we all thought it was just the way the sun was hitting the water, but it wasn't. I still don't know whose blood it was, but it was definitely real. I mean, there were some people swimming when it happened and that stuff never came out of their bathing suits!

Pharaoh was evidently not impressed, because he ordered the slaves to work harder.

God sent flies. It was unbelievable. They were everywhere. Jillions of flies.

Pharaoh made the slaves work harder.

Frogs were next. More frogs than you can imagine. It made everyone very jumpy (Ha Ha). Seriously, though, at least the frogs ate some of the flies.

Pharaoh made everyone work harder.

Locusts.

More work.

Caterpillars.

More work.

God killed Pharaoh's cattle.

Pharaoh made God's people work harder.

Now understand, God's people were pretty happy when I first went to Pharaoh. After laying down the law to Pharaoh the first time, I went back to the slave dormitory and they all sang, "For He's a Jolly Good Fellow." I was touched. But, hey, at the first sign of trouble, they were on me like white on rice! "Gee, thanks, Moses," they said. "Everything was okay until you showed up to help. Now we're working five times harder!"

Let me be the first to tell you, it was not a lot of fun. I tried telling God, "Hey, we've got a situation on our hands. These people are ticked!" But God was ticked, too. God, His people, Pharaoh . . . everybody was ticked—and I was right in the middle.

I don't want to go to four tablets for this letter (you try writing on a rock!), so I'll get to the point. After God brought some sickness and death, Pharaoh cried uncle and let everybody go. Now here is the cool part. He was so glad to get rid of us that he asked us to take everything. I mean everything—their gold, their jewelry, rocking chairs—we took it all. And... the former slaves were strong enough to carry it.

You see, Andy, all the extra work everyone had been doing was in God's plan after all. The whole deal was His way of killing two birds with one stone. A little pressure for Pharaoh on the one hand. And on the other, a kind of National Physical Fitness Program for us!

Hey, be assured. God really does have the best in mind for you. Sometimes His methods may seem a little crazy and we'd like Him to just get to the point, but it is His world, and we are His people. Time obviously doesn't mean the same thing to Him as it does to us. So be patient. . . . He can take what looks like the worst and make it the best. And He will.

Your friend,

Moses

Daniel Boone

"PIONEER"

...played a major role in the exploration of Kentucky. He founded and helped govern one of the first settlements—Boonesboro.

1734–1820

I had a coonskin cap when I was seven years old. Remember Fess Parker? Remember the song? "What a Boone, what a doer, what a dream-come-a-truer was he." But he wasn't just a television hero—Daniel Boone was a man (was a real man)! One of America's greatest frontiersmen, he has now become nothing short of a legend. Though an icon of endearing folklore, Boone was very much a real person who experienced the same trials in life as the rest of us. Fanciful stories from tradition make him out to be larger than life. The reality of the matter is that in most ways Daniel Boone was, in fact, larger than life. He epitomized the pioneer character and spirit that were requisite commodities for the early American settlers.

For most of us, trials don't include a daily existence on constant guard for our life. But the whack of the white man's ax and the crack of his rifle were heard by the Indians as a death knell, foretelling their ultimate doom. Daniel Boone guarded his own life and that of hundreds of settlers expanding into the unsurveyed wilderness. He was a veteran of the French and Indian wars, an American revolutionary patriot, and an inspiration to those carving their new lives in a new land. A skilled hunter, trapper, scout, and Indian fighter, Daniel Boone forged a path to the land of Kentucky through the Cumberland Gap. He was well acquainted with challenges, sorrows, defeat, and victory.

DANIEL BOONE

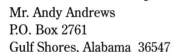

Mr. Andy Andrews
P.O. Box 2761
Gulf Shores, Alabama 36547

Dear Mr. Andrews,

My time of life was an exhilarating and thrilling one. Certainly it was a dangerous time, but I would have chosen no other time to abide on this earth if given an option. I realize now that my name and memory have been carried to the ends of America in every direction and incorporated into its history, indeed woven into the fabric of Old Glory herself by now. I was a loyal American from my beginnings. My family and I were Quakers. My grandfather had settled into the great land of Pennsylvania, living near Philadelphia. I had been all set up by good old William Penn for the spiritual and political equality of all men.

I was raised up in the wilderness around different tribes of Indians. I'd been familiar with Indians since childhood, as the Quakers were very cordial to them, and Quakers were equally well received by them. As a young boy, I tended my father's cattle herds while roaming the distant hills and valleys of Pennsylvania and beyond. My adolescent occupation acquainted me with the sharpened skills of an outdoorsman. I became a hunter, a horseman, an unerring marksman with a rifle and learned to live off the land, needing nothing from civilization. The education I received from nature was expansive, but of book learning I had very little. I was no scholar, but I was able to read and write to a satisfactory degree.

My frontier skills took me to the aid of England's General Braddock when he marched into the wilderness to defeat the French, who had rallied the Indian tribes against the colonies. I saw a fair share of death and destruction. I killed several Frenchmen and Indians in this campaign. I risked my life and tested the odds of leaving my wife and children as widow and orphans. But I came out of the campaign better for the ordeal. My skills, so sharpened in the wilderness as a youth, had proven themselves effective in securing my own survival and return to my family. It would not be the last time I'd be calling on these survival skills.

I had developed a reputation in the French and Indian wars which had made me a popular scout for the English in the defenses of various settlements and forts. My comrades began to feel I was somehow charmed because I always survived, nearly unscathed, in so many battles, while inflicting devastating casualties upon the French and the Indians. I did this as a service to my country. Just as much as any other soldier in any other American war, I lived in a time of national peril; not only from the French and Indians, but later from the English themselves. I learned to live with fear and doubt. It was a hard life, but it was a time to make heroes or cowards of either men or women—there was no middle course.

I had moved my family to the Yadkin River area of North Carolina. I spent years there while making my living as a trapper. I always felt crowded when I saw the land being too settled. I'd heard of a trapper's paradise in the land called Kentucky. Wanting to give my family a secure raising, I delayed my wanderlust for twelve years before I struck out to find this paradise beyond the farthest western borders of white civilization. The Yadkin was too crowded, and game was too scarce to properly provide for my family. I gathered five other trusted men, and we spent a year in Kentucky after finding our way 300 miles through the Cumberland Gap.

We trapped and hunted all year, until Indians took us captive and stole our furs. We escaped and stole them back again. We were recaptured, had our furs stolen again, and released. While in hiding, I trapped and hunted another year and made a good deal of potential profit. But again, the Indians found me and stole my living for the second year in a row. My tolerance for Indians faded rather quickly.

Soon, I was summoned by Richard Henderson of the Transylvania Company to help take settlers into the land of Kentucky to make another colony. I took the job and cut a 300-mile trail through the Cumberland Gap to Kentucky to lead a group of settlers to a town I called Boonesboro.

The American Revolutionary War was upon us. The English were now inciting the Indians into marauding the American settlements. I found myself in the middle of the frontier among Shawnee, Cherokee, Iroquois, and other hostile Indian tribes who began capturing, torturing, and killing white settlers almost at will. I became a captain in the American army, but as the crucial need of America's army was to be fighting on the Atlantic coast, no help could be sent to us. The settlers began to abandon Kentucky and flee east again. I was responsible for bringing them here, and I felt responsible for protecting them.

My fourteen-year-old daughter, Jemima, was kidnapped by hostile Shawnee Indians, with two other girls of about her age. My heart sank and I was terrified. I ran on foot for two days with a small group of men. We found the Indian band camped and unsuspecting. The girls were alive and well. We killed two Indians and the rest fled. My daughter and the other girls were unharmed. It was not so with my firstborn son, James. There was no warning, no sound, but the whirring of arrows as a small band of painted Shawnee Indians attacked my fourte-year-old son's camp at dawn upon Wallen's Ridge. Two twelve-year-old boys were killed instantly, and a grown man was killed by a tomahawk blow to his head. One man escaped with an arrow in his back, and another, Adam Washington, successfully hid and was the only witness to the savagery that followed.

My son, James, and his friend Henry Russel had been shot with arrows through their hips so that neither could move. Adam heard young James plead for his life. Soon, though, he was pleading for a merciful death. He got neither. The Indians tore out James' and Henry's fingernails; they gashed their faces bloody with their knives and gouged at their bodies, taking care not to inflict a fatal wound. The palms of the two boys were shredded in endless, futile attempts to turn aside the slashing blades. Finally, the work was done. The screaming stopped and the boys were dead. The Indians took their scalps and left a war club by their bodies, an act of bravado and challenge.

When I was told of the massacre, my wife, Rebeccah, gave me a sheepskin to wrap James' body. I rode back and found my son and the others. I buried them. I had given up or sold everything I had to settle this land of Kentucky. Now my son was dead. Was it worth it? Oh, the agony I experienced over that question! The remaining settlers had their livestock scattered and their courage sapped. Had I made the greatest mistake of my life by trying to settle this hostile country? This secret hour of mourning at Wallen's Ridge served to epitomize the untallied mortal cost of the westward expansion and part of my storm of perfection.

Beyond the epic drama in which a simple, semiliterate people force back the frontier with the doggedness of pine roots cracking granite so they can grow, beyond the mixture of blood and politics that fused the wilderness to the new nation—beyond the all that is this moment at Wallen's Ridge: a father sitting by the grave of his firstborn, a boy just turning into a man, who has been tortured to death. I sat there a long time, a lonely figure in deerskin dyed black, my eyes clouded by defeat and staring down at the fresh earth where my firstborn son and my dreams lay buried.

But I realized I had nothing to return to in North Carolina. Even if I was the only one left, I would not now leave Kentucky. I would not allow my son to die in vain. This sorrow, over time, renewed my resolve to settle this grand country of Kentucky. The settlers saw that I could personally identify with their fears and losses. It inspired their dreams again. They returned. Reinforcements came. We fought, cried, and lived together. And we realized our dreams of making a life on the frontier. In the end, I had been awarded large amounts of land in the new frontier. I had lived a life of my own choosing and enjoyed it to its fullest. I would not allow defeat to be the ultimate victor. I could be discouraged, but I would never be dissuaded from my path.

Yours Truly,

Daniel Boone

Daniel Boone

Wilbur Wright

"INVENTOR"

*...together with his brother, Orville,
invented and flew the first
practical airplane.*

1867–1912

The phenomenon of flight has intrigued humanity for centuries. For thousands of years, great men and women of learning had studied the science and art of flight in hopes of one day achieving the ability to soar on the winds of the world. For generations, fables, legends, and fantasies have been rooted in the prospect of flight. Indeed, this dream of achieving flight, though sought after as a precious treasure, had escaped the most talented and greatest minds the world could offer until a quirk in circumstance befell a young man in Ohio during the latter part of the nineteenth century.

It was not the day that Wilbur Wright found the "holy grail" by achieving powered flight with his brother, Orville. It was the day that Wilbur Wright's hopes and ambitions were dashed to pieces in a bizarre accident which made the difference in his life and redirected the once young, athletic, would-be professor's attentions toward the possibilities found in invention. On one fateful day at Kitty Hawk, South Carolina, Wilbur Wright accomplished with his brother what thousands of years of hopeful inventors had only dreamed of. The possibility of powered flight had been harnessed.

WILBUR WRIGHT
Dayton, Ohio

Mr. Andy Andrews
P.O. Box 2761
Gulf Shores, Alabama 36547

Dear Andy:

A storm of perfection; this phrase conveys a true paradox. Nevertheless, anyone who has traveled the road which leads to great accomplishments has certainly endured one or more along the way. It is an irony of life which, when understood, reveals great hope even in the midst of the most dismal of circumstances, and facilitates the building of great strength of character to the one who persists through it.

My father was a bishop of the Church of the United Brethren in Christ. Early on, he instilled in me a love of reading and creativity. I became a voracious reader and developed an excellent memory. I dreamed of one day becoming a teacher, perhaps even a professor. This pleased my parents, who began preparations to secure a Yale University education for me.

I had earned excellent grades in high school, particularly in Greek, Latin, geometry, natural philosophy, geology, and composition. I also had been an outstanding athlete, who excelled in gymnastics, running, and football. I was a determined young man who believed all of life waited for me with nothing but the promise of absolute success.

Then, as an unexpected tempest can violently shake foundations previously believed to be secure, my storm of perfection suddenly began. I was nineteen years old, playing a game on skates while on a frozen artificial lake near Dayton, Ohio. A bat accidentally flew out of the hands of another participant and struck me. I was knocked to the ground by the impact, but apparently not badly injured. This incident, however, somehow precipitated a number of physical disorders.

I soon began experiencing nervous heart palpitations and digestive disorders. My now serious physical ailments precluded the realization of a Yale education. That dream was now beyond my grasp. A permanent teaching post would require a college diploma, and in view of my uncertain health, that would probably be time and money wasted. My dream was shattered upon the ice on that fateful day when I was nineteen years old.

Unable to chart a new course that appealed to me, I fell into a depression born of frustration, indecision, and self-doubt. I resolved to remain at home to care for my ailing mother. I remained at home for three years, suffering feelings of vulnerability while watching friends leave home, launch careers, and establish families of their own. For three long years I remained prey to feelings of weakness and a growing sense that I might be incapable of coping with an ordinary, independent life. I withdrew into myself.

In time, by means of fortitude, I was able to attempt a new beginning. I began to realize that perceiving the merits of others while seeing only my own weaknesses was just as debilitating and paralyzing, if not more so, than my physical impairments. While struggling to overcome fits of depression during my young manhood, I developed enormous self-confidence in the process.

I regained my courage while I refined a new dream. I associated myself with my brother, Orville, an optimist by nature, and ventured into creative business enterprises. We opened a bicycle shop and began inventing new devices for bicycles and other mechanical equipment. This worked to further advance my self-assuredness and confidence. It stimulated creativity and allowed me to believe there could be something else awaiting me on the horizon, perhaps something bigger and better than I would have ever been able to attain had I become a teacher rather than an inventor.

Orville and I went on to invent the airplane. I need not expound upon the significance of our success in achieving powered flight, nor the impact our device was to forever have upon human history. I will say, however, that because of the boldness I developed while overcoming the setbacks of my young life, I was able to become a very outgoing and gifted public speaker.

I was cool, aloof, and controlled as I sold the idea of the airplane to a world that viewed this advancement as nothing more than a novelty for the first years after its conception.

I must now ponder what I, and the world, may have missed had not the course of my life been altered in the storm of perfection. What I then looked upon as a grave misfortune, I now view as a splendid turn of events.

Very sincerely,

Wilbur Wright

"I count him braver who overcomes
his desires than him who conquers
his enemies; for the hardest
victory is the victory over self."

Aristotle

Robert Fulton

"INVENTOR"

...designed the first efficient steamboat.
Through his invention,
he opened a new era of
power-driven navigation.

1765–1815

Fulton was one of the greatest American inventors and entrepreneurs in history. He was a bold imaginer, whose relentless quest for mechanical and engineering advancements rendered a harvest of inventions and ideas ahead of their time. At the time of his death, forty-nine, Fulton was declared a national benefactor. He was a symbol of America's dream of leading the technological revolution and had made unprecedented contributions toward establishing our naval and mechanical superiority, on a global scale. Catastrophe sometimes has a redeeming aspect. This was evident in Fulton, as many of his inventions came as a result of national needs recognized after the American revolutionary war.

Robert Fulton designed the first efficient steamboat, catapulting American naval and commercial capabilities into a position of world leadership. This had finally made the American navy a force to be respected by every nation. Fulton's forward thinking excited controversy and made him the target of envious colleagues who shared his quest for invention. Fulton's novelties ranged from devising an operable submarine to the invention of the Roman Candle, an air gun, a lead pencil, and a fishing boat with mechanical paddles. Ironically, however, Fulton's first real forte was that of a painter. His employment as a sketch artist later helped him demonstrate his ideas in pictures. This ushered in the concept of blueprints for various types of manufacturers.

ROBERT FULTON

Mr. Andy Andrews
P.O. Box 2761
Gulf Shores, Alabama 36547

Dear Mr. Andrews,

Here's to the foolish recluses; absorbed in their own dreams, labeled as fools, and given over to the pursuit of making their ideas manifest within the realm of reality. Indeed, were it not for such creative people, willing to accept their negative stereotypes as kooks, eccentrics, and fools, while casting aside with reckless abandon everything which might deter them from completing their self-assigned tasks, we would have remained without the wheel, hand tools, the printing press, electric lighting, the steam engine, and many other great industrial advances.

Had I believed all the naysayers and the narrow-minded people who incorporated my surroundings, instead of staying focused on my own determination of purpose, seafarers might still be rowing their way across the Atlantic. Inventors such as Franklin, Edison, and the Wright brothers are now justly remembered as pioneers. But while we carried on with our endeavors, before anyone realized the possibilities or potential of our creations, we endured scathing insults and ridicule. I am glad to know now that my "stupid" idea of employing the power of a steam engine to create the first efficient steamboat has joined the ranks of other "stupid" ideas like the light bulb, the airplane, and the computer.

It is simply human nature, I suppose, for people to be so skeptical of novel thinking. Change is not easy to accept. It is far more difficult to promote. In my time, there were many needs to be met; many functions which could be carried out with the proper device if such an item could be created. I had thought of many ways to address these needs through the inventions of functional devices. My largest handicap was the fact that everything I had come up with was new. In the eyes of politicians, financial sponsors, and society in general, "new" equated to unorthodox, risky, foreign, and uncomfortable. The money required to manufacture my prototypes and unbuilt ideas was therefore extremely difficult to lay hold of.

I will not attempt to hide my own personality flaws as I write to you. While I possessed a clear and promising vision, I also was a man of fierce pride. I knew better than anyone that my inventions would work. In the face of scorn and disbelief, I was forced to develop an overcoming spirit that consumed criticism as its own fuel. It drove my determination to prove my points. Because of such continual rejection, I spent many years without my ideas being recognized or employed. Surely I had an abundant fuel supply in criticism, but some recognition was absolutely necessary for me, not only professionally, but emotionally as well. I would not receive it for many years, but it did come. It did . . . come.

I became incredibly frustrated that when change was imminent, and when through long study, application, and expense, I rose to the challenge to meet such a need, there were so many who would strip me of my due credit and income in their efforts to steal my ideas. I had been falsely accused of stealing the inventions of less ruthless and grasping predecessors.

The truth was that I had consulted with great scientific minds of the day in an honest and open effort to brainstorm the possibilities of new inventions and ideas. Too many times these colleagues attempted to undermine me by trying to patent my creations as their own inventions. When I took appropriate steps to prevent this from happening, I was openly accused of the same wrongdoing by the perpetrators themselves. My efforts to litigate these matters was a drain on my emotions, mental capacities, and finances. It also took away precious time which I needed to expend upon the development and testing of my ever-expanding host of inventions.

Fortunately for me, and in the long run for everyone, there were the honest and upright inventors as well as the crooked. Benjamin Franklin was undoubtedly the foremost inventor of the day. I had consulted with him on several occasions and always came away edified and inspired. His motivation spurred me toward maintaining high expectations of myself and to continue to dare to create and to think. I realize how much I owe to Franklin and others like him. I see clearly that anyone who achieves great things is obliged to become such a mentor to others. Reciprocally, anyone who wishes to overcome and reach great levels of achievement is obliged to find such a mentor for themselves.

The fear of meeting the opposition of envy, or the frugality of ignorance, is, no doubt, the frequent cause of preventing many ingenious men from ushering opinions into the world, which may deviate from the common practice. Hence, for want of energy, the young idea is shackled with timidity, and a useful thought is buried in the impenetrable gloom of eternal oblivion. The adventurer must therefore arm himself with fortitude to meet the attacks of illiberality and prejudice, determined to yield to nothing but superior reason.

There is also a secret pride which urges many to conceal their speculative inquiries, rather than meet criticism, or not be thought the first in their favorite pursuit; ever anxious to claim the merit of invention, they cannot brook the idea of having their work dissected and the minute parts attributed to the genius of other men. It takes courage, and is necessary for the benefit of all, that the mechanic should sit down among levers, screws, wedges, wheels, etc. Like a poet among the letters of the alphabet, considering them as the exhibition of his thoughts, in which a new arrangement transmits a new idea to the world.

Everyone in this world, no matter what they have put their hand to, will experience opposition and fear. It lies within a prison to overcome these things, although it will be a painful and perhaps long endeavor. My storm of perfection came in the form of rejection, misunderstanding, lack of sponsorships, and betrayal by colleagues. All of these vanished after I had finally overcome through persistence. I enjoyed the favor and recognition of men and of financial abundance. More important to me, however, I saw my ideas and inventions put to the tasks for which I had created them.

From my beginnings, I had been endowed with a creative mind and a sense of enterprise. I had to develop later, however, a great buoyancy of spirit and a self-generated optimism, impervious to criticism, to carry me onward through all the many obstacles I encountered. I encourage others to do likewise, as their efforts—anchored by persistence—will reap greater rewards than they can now imagine.

Sincerely,

Robert Fulton

Robert Fulton

Dwight D. Eisenhower

"MILITARY LEADER/ PRESIDENT"

...was Allied Supreme Commander in WW II. His popularity secured him election as the thirty-fourth president of the United States.

1890–1969

Vision is the tool that charts the course of our destiny. Dwight Eisenhower was a visionary, with a true sense of purpose, not only for himself, but for America. He was what our country needed in the midst of World War II. History has recorded him as one of the greatest military leaders of the world. His achievements as commander in chief of the American armed forces during this time helped to bring a swift end to the dark, oppressive powers attempting to dominate the world.

Politicians generally prompt strong feelings in people. There were those who disagreed with Eisenhower's policies as they related to the general administration of this country. However, the phrase "I like Ike" continued to ring through the corridors of a country as our fighting troops poured onto the shores of foreign lands, and returned again with victory secured.

Dwight D. Eisenhower

Mr. Andy Andrews
P.O. Box 2761
Gulf Shores, Alabama 36547

Dear Andy,

When I was a high school boy, I wandered into the offices of the Abilene News one day. There, I picked up a book belonging to the editor. This book told of the thrilling adventures of one of the world's greatest military leaders—Hannibal. I was awed by the story of how he crossed the Alps with elephants and fought the Italians for fifteen years. I was fascinated with military history, devouring Gibbon's "Decline and Fall of the Roman Empire" and reading biographies of Lee, Grant, Washington, and Stonewall Jackson. I was so fascinated with history that my classmates at Abilene High School prophesied that one day I'd be a college professor of history. That prophecy was a bit off-center. I never taught history. I did, however, play a part in making it. My real name, of course, is Dwight David, but my friends just called me "Ike."

After being accepted to West Point, my big dream of a military career became only a glimmer. I became afraid that I'd never graduate. School, except history, had never been a passion of mine, and my grades were going from bad to worse.

Somewhere along the line, I had a turning point when I asked myself the question: What do I really want? Well, I wanted a career in the military. Did I like school? No. Did I want to study? No. I wanted a career in the military.

The only way to obtain the kind of career I wanted in the military was to graduate from West Point; therefore, I learned one of life's huge lessons: Sometimes we do things we don't want to do in order to obtain the results we desire.

I never became a great scholar. I graduated sixty-first from the top in a class of one hundred sixty-four—hardly leadership material. That tough time as a student, however, helped me achieve something infinitely more important than high grades. I achieved vision. My struggle for passing grades also instilled in me an attention for detail. Both virtues were called into play the day we invaded Normandy.

At that point, I commanded an army greater than the combined infantries of Napoleon, Julius Caesar, Hannibal, and Charlamagne. My fleet of ships was greater than the combined navies of Nelson, Hawkins, Drake, Admiral Dewey, and John Paul Jones. My assembly of air power was greater than previously could have been imagined.

My ability to plan to the last detail was a deciding factor in our success. For example, eight hundred typewritten pages were required to plan only the Navy's part in the invasion. One complete set of their orders and maps weighed three hundred pounds. Was the detail necessary? I'm not certain. Were the results worth the effort? Yes.

Historians have noted that besides my attention to detail, the vision I held for the successful movement of allied troops was, in reality, the crowning blow in the defeat of Nazi Germany. That amazes me still! It is incredible to think that 300 million people in Western Europe were granted a degree of safety because of the vision of one leader.

It is more incredible, however, to note that my powers of vision were developed not only while I was a poor student, but because I was one!

Sincerely,

Dwight D. Eisenhower

Dwight Eisenhower

"He that does good to another
does good also to himself...."

Seneca

Clara Barton

"HUMANITARIAN"

…founder of the American Red Cross. She was decorated with the German Iron Cross for her efforts in treating injured soldiers in the Franco-Prussian War.

1821–1912

Clara Barton was a noted American humanitarian. Her first career was that of school teacher, but she went on to fill an important post in the U.S. Patent Office in Washington, D.C., and later volunteered, during the Civil War, to help soldiers at the front, offering nursing skills and bringing needed supplies to them. President Lincoln thought most highly of her, backing her in her efforts and encouraging her after the war to find missing soldiers in action.

Perhaps her greatest achievement was in bringing about the establishment of the American Red Cross. Later, she was instrumental in seeing to it that this organization aided victims not only during wartime, but in peacetime tragedies such as floods, fires, and famines—work that the Red Cross continues to this day.

At the time of her death, a newspaper editorial read: "Clara Barton was more than brave. She devoted her life to humanity. She was one of the most useful of women, self-sacrificing to a degree, generous to a fault. Health and fortune she devoted to her great cause."

CLARA BARTON
INTERNATIONAL RED CROSS

Mr. Andy Andrews
P.O. Box 2761
Gulf Shores, Alabama 36547

Dear Mr. Andrews:

It is always a pleasure for a person like me to have the opportunity to put forth information on my life's interests and goals, inasmuch as it has always been my deepest wish to serve humankind.

Educated at home in rural Massachusetts, I later became a teacher and came to manage rural schoolhouses, with students of all ages in one room. At the time, this was a major challenge for someone as shy as I was. However, my interests lay far beyond a rural schoolhouse. I wanted to serve the larger world outside.

But many trials were placed in my path. Ill health plagued me throughout my life. As a young woman, I contracted malaria, which, even when cured, left a basic weakness in my system. I think that only sheer willpower plus my faith in God were able to sustain me and enable me to overcome.

I needed all the faith I could muster, for heartbreaking obstacles met me at every turn. Although I was the first woman ever appointed as a clerk in the patent office in Washington, and my work was highly valued, I was asked to resign when the political climate changed.

I was heartbroken. What was I to do? By now, I was thirty-six years old. My career seemed ruined by overwork, antifeminist attitudes toward me on the job, and the political spoils system. The stress of this situation made further inroads on my health: My eyes and throat constantly troubled me, and I could barely function.

But a national calamity arose which inspired me to overcome my own problems. It was the time of the terrible Civil War, and President Abraham Lincoln needed help for the war effort. I volunteered and actually went to the front to aid the soldiers, although I was by this time almost forty years old. I was never a professional nurse, but I put all my heart and soul into this work. I tore up my own sheets to make bandages for the soldiers and brought baskets of food to them which I paid for with my own money. In fact, I came to be known as the "Angel of the Battlefield."

I also had useful organizational talents: I could think straight, plan carefully, and act boldly. Thus I devised means of caring for the wounded nearer the battle so that many of them need not die unnecessarily while awaiting medical attention.

After the war, with the encouragement and backing of President Lincoln, I helped search for missing prisoners of war. Later I helped establish hospitals in Europe during the Franco-Prussian War and was very proud to be honored with the Iron Cross of Germany.

But later, seeking success as a public speaker, I, at one such engagement, lost my voice when I reached the podium. My career as a public speaker was at an end.

Furthermore, whenever I found myself without a project, my health would collapse. At a particularly dark time in my life, I had to enter a sanitarium. There followed the worst years of my life. My beloved sister Sally had died, I lacked a passionate goal, and it was as if my entire system, both physical and psychic, had given up. Body and soul were stricken.

My doctors could only call it nervous prostration. For a long period, I could not stand unaided and averaged less than two hours' sleep every night for almost a year.

I was to spend almost ten years in the sanitarium in the town of Dansville, New York, where I was protected from knowing very much about the events in the world.

But even during my period of recuperation, I felt the need to be involved, to contribute to humankind's progress. It was during this time, the darkest of my life, in which I founded the International Red Cross.

This was the culmination of my life's work. During my service, I was able to establish guidelines so that the Red Cross could serve victims of peacetime disasters as well as victims of war. I feel that this was a profound advance; it enabled thousands of people to benefit from aid—medical, housing, needed supplies, food—which they would not otherwise have been able to obtain.

Interestingly, the people who have been helped in some way by the efforts of the Red Cross might have been left to their own devices if not for the darkest hours of my life. Ten years in a sanitarium is nothing I would have chosen as a path to enlightenment, but for me, it turned out to be exactly that! Millions have now been affected in a positive way because of one person's idea, an idea which was born of pain.

Best Wishes,

Clara Barton

Clara Barton

Hernán Cortés

"EXPLORER"

…Sixteenth-century Spaniard who conquered the Aztec Empire. He later built Mexico City.

1485–1547

Burn the boats! It's one of my favorite sayings because of the absolute commitment it calls for. The phrase came from Hernán Cortés himself. Cortés, the great conquistador of Spain, was the commander responsible for the subjugation of Mexico in the 1500s. Many attempts had been made to conquer the mighty armies of Mexico and to claim the land and its great treasures for other countries. No one had ever been successful. In the prior attempts, there was always the possibility of retreat. When Cortés sailed his fleet to the shores of Mexico, he gave the command to "Burn the boats!" It meant that he and his army would accomplish what they set out to do or die trying. There was no back door, no retreat, no second thought. This bold action indeed gave a more complete motivation to himself and his army to succeed.

Boldness is what is called for and too often missing in many of our endeavors today. The willingness to allow for turning back will sabotage any effort for success. Cortés was a man who had learned from defeat. Defeat had been his greatest teacher, and without it, he would never have been able to learn the lessons he needed to reach his ultimate victory.

Hernán Cortés

Mr. Andy Andrews
P.O. Box 2761
Gulf Shores, Alabama 36547

Mr. Andrews,

In February of 1519, I set sail on the final leg of a voyage that was to bring about the fulfillment of a dream. This voyage was to deliver my ships and crew onto the shores of southern Mexico, on the Yucatan Peninsula. There we would take the world's richest treasure. A treasure of gold, silver, and jewels that had been held by the same army for more than 600 years.

I was confident. Never mind the fact that army after army had failed to take the treasure. I would succeed. I would take the ultimate prize of every explorer in the world. This treasure was my holy grail.

My confidence was born of knowledge gained from failure. At the time, failure was the essence of my reputation. There were three glorious missions I had attempted in the past. All had ended in failure.

The first two never reached a destination at all. The men retreated and our ships returned to Spain. The third mission, an occupation of northern Mexico, ended in disaster when three fourths of my troops were massacred.

But that winter day in February so long ago, I was in excellent spirits. I had in my command eleven vessels containing 500 soldiers, 100 sailors, and sixteen horses. The tragedies I had experienced in the past had been for a purpose. I was certain that I had learned an important lesson and was just as certain of success.

My first two failures had occurred because of doubt and lack of leadership. I hadn't spent much time among the crew, and I didn't fully articulate my team concept for success. I also allowed different groups of workers free communication with each other all over the ship. This, I now realized, had been a mistake. The helmsmen talked to the soldiers about how long it had been since we'd seen land. The cook talked to the junior officers about his concerns of running out of food. Soon, this crossing of bad information had everyone doubting me and the success of our mission. They demanded to return home, and, under threat of death, I complied. The disaster in northern Mexico was much the same story. The men had talked so much to each other about how fierce the enemy was that when the enemy actually showed up, they were paralyzed with fear. We were routed by an army shooting arrows and throwing rocks. Six hundred of my men died with muskets in their hands. Two hundred of the muskets had never been fired.

My quest for the world's richest treasure would end differently. To insure a successful outcome, I did three things to prepare my men.

1) Each day, I spoke to my crews of victory. The leaders kept the vision of a bright future in their everyday thoughts. Over and over again, we talked of how life would be lived as possessors of the world's richest treasure.

2) I instituted a rule of no cross-grouping between crews. We worked as a unit, but the helmsmen and the cook were not to discuss their specific jobs or concerns they might have. The sailors and soldiers discussed their problems only with me. Naysayers were isolated from the main group. We never had a challenge of fear, and in fact, the enthusiasm seemed to build for our task ahead.

3) As we landed in a rocky cove, I knew the third part of my plan was at hand. After several days, regaining our land legs, I gathered the men around me and uttered the three words that guaranteed our success.

"Burn the boats!" At first there was confusion. "Why should we burn the boats?" one of the soldiers cried out. "They are our only means of retreat," said another. "There will be no retreat," I replied. "A retreat is for a beaten army. You will not be beaten. Burn the boats," I commanded again. "If we are to go home—let it be in their boats."

As history records, the men fought well and we took the treasure. Yes, it was the first time it had been taken in 600 years, but it was a victory provided by failure. Without my embarrassing failures, I might never have learned the principles of success so crucial to my historical campaign.

Keep the vision of a successful future.
Eliminate doubt and discord.
Remember that retreat is not an option.

With best wishes,

Hernán Cortés

Susan B. Anthony

"REFORMER"

*...led the struggle to
gain the vote for women.
She died before the
19th amendment was adopted.*

1820–1906

Susan Brownell Anthony, better known as Susan B. Anthony—and later in life, simply as Susan B.—was a renowned reformer whose name became synonymous with the women's suffrage movement in the United States. Steeped in her family's Quaker faith, which emphasized the importance of equal rights for men and women, Anthony fought tirelessly for women's rights throughout her life and also was in the forefront of the antislavery and temperance movements. In 1851, after meeting women's movement leader Elizabeth Cady Stanton, Anthony focused primarily on that cause.

Although she died fourteen years before the passage of the 19th Amendment to the U.S. Constitution—which gave women the right to vote—Anthony never lost faith in the eventual achievement of that goal. She also predicted that a woman would someday be elected president of the United States. When Anthony's face was pictured on newly minted $1 coins beginning in 1979, it marked the first time a woman was so honored on coins that were earmarked for general circulation.

SUSAN B. ANTHONY

Mr. Andy Andrews
P.O. Box 2761
Gulf Shores, Alabama 36547

Dear Mr. Andrews,

On August 26, 1920, the 19th Amendment to the constitution was adopted. That stroke of the pen finally gave women in America the right to vote. Many people at the time called that particular piece of legislation the Susan B. Anthony Amendment. The title, of course, flatters me. It would have been more flattering, however, if I'd been alive to see it happen.

Let me explain. I invested the greater portion of my life, over half a century, to a cause I know to be worthy and correct. The entire tenure of my fight was waged while enduring ridicule, abuse, opposition from the press, derision from the pulpit, and disinterest from women themselves.

In 1906, the year of my passing from earth, the women's suffrage movement was at a standstill. All the arguments had been advanced, all the facts had been presented, and the question had ceased to be news. Like Napoleon at Waterloo, I was a splendid failure. In fact, my obituary stated that I had "failed in my lifelong quest." Quite the contrary is actually true. Storms and their following perfections rarely *happen according to our timetable, and the perfection part of the equation sometimes occurs in time. I recently discovered that the Lord doesn't keep the same kind of clock that most of us do. Neither is He under any obligation to tell us what He is doing in our lives.*

Please understand. If I had been working for Susan B. Anthony and her chance to mark a ballot, I would have been disappointed, possibly angry with the Almighty, because that opportunity was never presented me.

But as it stands, I am ecstatic. I was working for womankind. I won. Women vote today because of what we started.

My death was actually a new beginning. New leaders read my obituary, read about the storms I went through, and took up the banner. Fourteen years later, as the amendment was signed, I applauded from my balcony.

If you are struggling with a cause that is bigger than you, rest assured—your work will not be in vain. The perfection you seek may elude your vision for a while, but the results of your work will benefit generations. Remember, failure is not possible—because there are no time limits.

Yours truly,

Susan B. Anthony

Susan B. Anthony

"Too many people are thinking
of security instead of opportunity."

James F. Byrnes

Sir Winston Churchill

"STATESMAN"

... is best known for his courageous leadership as prime minister of England during WW II. He was Great Britain's greatest twentieth-century diplomat.

1874–1965

Being a national leader responsible for uplifting your country while bombs are ripping the countryside to pieces has an incredible burden. Winston Churchill shouldered such a responsibility with remarkable courage and poise. Churchill's wisdom and tact held his country together and emboldened them to march forward in the face of a brutal enemy barrage of firepower. His understanding and ability to know just the right thing to say in just the right way left all the allied countries of World War II inspired. Could it be that this great man, too, was a man of failure?

Churchill's storms of perfection were exactly the reason why he was the right man for the job at just the right time. He knew the sting of public ridicule and had even been forced to resign from the admiralty of England for supporting a disastrous campaign at Galipoli and having endured other naval difficulties. Hard times were Churchill's playing field. He had grown accustomed to fighting for every inch of turf, respect, or support he'd ever received. His skills were sharpened by adversity and were consequently razor sharp during perhaps the darkest hours in England's history.

WINSTON CHURCHILL

Andy Andrews
P. O. Box 2761
Gulf Shores, Alabama 36547

Dear Mr. Andrews,

Once again, it begins. Even now, in my mind's eye, I can hear the fearful explosions that signal the falling of new Nazi bombs on London, Liverpool, and the rest of the British Isles. These fearsome thunderclaps are soon joined by the piercing wail of the air raid sirens, the drum-like beat of the anti-aircraft guns, and the ghostly glow of the searchlights, the sum total of which resembles a deadly circus only the devil himself could appreciate. The Battle of Britain has begun its nightly performance.

Meanwhile, underneath the chaos and destruction in the streets, the brave citizens of the city sit in the depths of the London Underground—rich and poor, black and white, young and old huddled together in the darkness. No one knows if their homes and families will still remain when the bombing is over. We are a small nation, Mr. Andrews, not much larger than your own state of Alabama, yet we were standing alone against the full, unfettered fury of the greatest war machine the world had ever encountered.   The United States was our ideological ally, but had not yet entered the fight. France had already fallen to Hitler's legions, as had the rest of Europe. Only England stood unbowed and unconquered.

And so, night after night, the brave people of Great Britain could be found singing and praying together, testing their will and resolve against German buzz bombs, aeroplanes, and V-2 rockets. Overhead, their sons, husbands, and fathers fought a desperate and exhaustive air battle in their outnumbered Hurricanes and Spitfires. And they did not yield. It was their sacrifice and bravery of which I spoke when I said: "Never in the field of human conflict has so much been owed by so many to so few."   But it was the courage of the British people that finally convinced Adolf Hitler that he would never break the back of England. It was their indomitable spirit that held on until American help could arrive and beat the Nazi horde back to Berlin.

Mr. Andrews, I must tell you that a terrible price was paid during the "storms" of the London Blitz. Thousands lost their lives or those of loved ones, and tens of thousands more lost all that they possessed in the rubble of the streets. But these same courageous could emerge from that dark nightmare to rebuild their lives and reload their guns. The determination and guts of the British people inspired an entire free world, and tyranny was defeated as a result. To measure the importance of this decision to persevere, consider this: Had the citizens of England chosen to give up, to surrender, as so many nations had done before them, our world might be a very different place.

In 1941, I made what was certainly one of the shorter speeches of my career at the Harrow School. In it I stated: "Never give in! Never, never, never, never—in nothing great and small—large and petty. Never give in except to convictions of honour and good sense." If there is one idea, one scrap of thought that I can convey to your readers, Mr. Andrews, it is simply "fight on." When the odds are steadfastly against you, when there seems to be no one there to cheer you on, when defeat and surrender seem to be the only options, fight on. It is at those times when the night seems darkest that we discover what true character is; and it is invariably at those times that the sun chooses to shine brightest. It is the simplest lesson I can give on the subject of success, in any endeavor. It saved my nation, and perhaps the world.

Fight on!

Winston Churchill

"Do not associate with a
man given to anger;
or go with a hot-tempered man,
lest you learn his ways."

Proverbs 22:24–25

P.T. Barnum
"ENTREPRENEUR"

...together with James Anthony Bailey, formed the world-famous Barnum & Bailey Circus. He was one of the first American entrepreneurs to realize the money-making potential found in publicity.

1810–1891

Phineas Taylor Barnum was born one day late, July 5, 1810. He would have preferred that the country ignite fireworks and celebrate coast to coast to commemorate the entrance of the Greatest Showman on Earth. But, as nature would have it, he missed it by twenty-four hours. The name Phineas was well placed. Its biblical meaning is "brazen mouth." P.T.'s maternal grandfather had the most influence on the boy in his formative years. The bespectacled, mop-headed, boisterous old man dearly loved his grandson and spent all of his time and lump sugar on him. In P.T.'s own words, "My grandfather would go farther, wail longer, work harder, and contrive deeper to carry out a practical joke than for anything else under heaven." This model served Phineas well in his later years.

His father died when he was fifteen years old, leaving the family bankrupt and Phineas as the sole supporter. He began work as a clerk in a nearby general store, where his ability for promotion and a vision of broader horizons became evident. Soon after leaving the clerking profession, P.T. Barnum became known as "The Greatest Showman on Earth" as he put tour after tour together, displaying oddities from around the world. General Tom Thumb; Jumbo the Elephant; and Chan & Eng, the original Siamese Twins, were just a few of Barnum's long-running promotions. In 1881 he joined with rival showman James Anthony Bailey to found the famous Barnum & Bailey Circus and change entertainment forever. P.T. Barnum died in 1891. World famous and respected for his accomplishments in removing social barriers against entertainment and his use of curiosity and sensation in promotion, he was indeed The Greatest Showman on Earth.

P.T. BARNUM

Mr. Andy Andrews
P.O. Box 2761
Gulf Shores, Alabama 36547

Dear Andy,

I hope you realize that to ask a showman—in my particular case, *the showman*—to expound on his life and times is to open floodgates of promotion and exaggeration. In fact, there is nothing I like more than the telling of the tale. More correctly put, embellishing a tale in a way that attracts crowds. The bigger the better. My odd vocation began as I was hard at work in my grandfather's store in Bethel, Connecticut. A customer entered the store, remarking that he'd just seen a curious sight. A dog of ordinary size, but with two tails. One of which was over three feet long! When I inquired if the dog was still in the area and if he might be for sale, the customer said yes, he was close by and could most likely be purchased for a few dollars. I saw opportunity! I saw crowds! I saw money! Excitedly, I took off my apron, hurried out the door, and mounted my horse. The customer stepped out onto the porch and gave one last bit of information: the dog had been exiting a tanning yard, and one of the tails was a cow tail that he carried in his mouth. I dismounted somewhat less enthusiastically amid the laughter of friends, but never lost my feel for opportunity found in the unusual.

It was July 1835 when my destiny came calling in the form of one Coley Bartram. Into the store he walked with a bit of news that changed my life and the history of showmanship forever. He spoke of a woman called Joice Heth. This woman was reported to be 161 years old and to have been the nursemaid of President George Washington during his infancy. The gentleman currently in charge of Joice Heth was not a true showman and was eager to return to his home state of Tennessee. He was looking for a buyer. I was hungry for bigger and better opportunity. We haggled over the $3,000 asking price, and when the dust cleared, we agreed on $1,000 for the Joice Heth Show. To secure the purchase, I talked the seller into a purchase-option arrangement for $500—It was all the money I had in the world! Next, I convinced my wife of the solidity of the plan. Then I sold my partner my half of the grocery store to get the remaining money necessary to finalize the deal. In a few short days I became a showman. P.T. Barnum's career was launched! Careful planning, staging, and promotion turned this 161-year-old woman of exceptional mind and wit into a small industry. Then the inevitable happened. Joice Heth finally went on to meet her Maker. True to my word, I allowed a famous surgeon friend to perform a post-mortem examination. Dr. David L. Rogers returned findings that shocked and frightened me. Joice Heth was no more than 80 years of age at the time of her death. The scandal hit the paper with the headline: "HOAX!" I'll tell you, I was devastated. I had done my research and was convinced the records I had were authentic. The stories continued as I carefully watched what I fully expected to be the end of P.T. Barnum, Showman. I literally made plans to move my family and seek other career paths. I was anxious about my future, to put it mildly. Certainly, at best, this phase of my life was over . . . I thought.

What actually happened was astounding! As the allegations continued to fly and the story grew, a strange promotional phenomenon was born. The suspected hoax became a part of the promotional fabric of the Joice Heth story. In other words, it increased the value of the show! Once I realized what was occurring, I was able to move the excitement and conflict into other shows that attracted huge paying crowds who discussed endlessly their authenticity—or lack thereof! Jumbo the Elephant, the Mermaid from Feejee, the Cardiff Giant, and many others, some real, some unreal, all fun, were in reality a product of Joice Heth. You see, I learned important lessons on several levels with Joice. First, things are not always what they seem in regard to what people would have you believe in business. Second, things are not always what they seem in regard to our emotions. I had been misled in the case of Joice Heth's age. I was taken! But my negative emotions—fear, dread, shame, guilt—nearly blinded me to the opportunity that ultimately led to the creation of the modern circus. What if I had followed my initial emotions out of town? What if I had heeded my feelings of being frightened into another career? I'd have probably died as a store clerk in a small Midwestern town. Nothing to be ashamed of . . . but certainly not the exciting life that lay before P.T. Barnum!

Keep your eyes open and a firm grip on your emotions. Think with your head in matters of business and with your heart in matters of compassion and fun. Then, Andy, I believe you will find life to be a circus!

Always your showman friend,

P T Barnum

P.T. Barnum

Captain James Cook

"EXPLORER"

...famous for his three great voyages of exploration in the South Pacific Ocean. He also navigated the North American coastal waters.

1728–1779

James Cook was only fifty-one years old when he was killed by natives of the Sandwich Islands in 1779. By that time, the great Captain Cook had already made his permanent mark on history as one of the most famous seafaring explorers of all time. The wild and vast uncharted lands were an alluring prize which called Cook to the sea. The threat to a sailor's life in those days was constant. With an unchainable spirit, Captain Cook inspired his crew to sail beyond all known waters and to touch the shores of new civilizations.

The discovery of previously unknown people, exotic places, and the seeking of all things was an excitement too tempting for Cook to resist. The difficulty of keeping up his crew's spirits was always a challenge. Cook's daring in the face of threatening seas, hostile new civilizations, and near mutinous crews was rewarded by the discovery of many new lands and maritime routes. He was lauded as a national hero for his bold expeditions and prosperous discoveries.

JAMES COOK

Mr. Andy Andrews
P.O. Box 2761
Gulf Shores, Alabama 36547

Dear Andy,

I was destined to be a captain and explorer; my temperament would have accepted nothing less. For you see, I believe movement is freedom. In movement I have been able to realize my innermost nature; to remain at home would have felt like captivity. In the 1700s sea travel was treacherous, with violent seas, unpredictable winds, poor directional instruments, and terminal diseases, but the adventure called to my soul.

I was fortunate enough to make three voyages to the Pacific Ocean, enjoying the discoveries of new frontiers. On my first voyage, our death rate was excessively high due to scurvy and the bloody flux. My second voyage was probably most noteworthy, but less than perfect, if you were to read my log. The goal of this expedition was to find the fabled southern continent, Terra Australis, thought to be a part of Africa. The second goal was to change diet and living conditions to the point where death on the seas due to disease was the exception rather than the norm.

Two ships were taken on this trip, the *Resolution*, which I commanded, and the *Adventure*, which accompanied us. We had difficulties manning these ships because the "lower-deck buzz" was that this voyage was going into waters no man knew, icy and interminable waste at the end of the world. I paid the men well; I intended to feed them well and keep them out of harm's way as best I could. I hired on a "real cook" and brought aboard proper foods to keep our diet wholesome and well rounded. I insisted on clean living quarters. Whatever I could do to keep this ship disease-free, I would do. Sick seamen are not of use in dire weather and tough conditions.

We set out for waters only a nuclear-powered submarine or massive ice-breaker should brave. The Antarctic is a great frozen land fringed by iceberg-littered pack and surrounded for the whole girth of the world by tempestuous seas. We found this out via on-the-job training! Our path was blocked by an endless zone of solid ice and poor visibility. We were surrounded by a maze of loose pieces of nasty floes, growlers, and icebergs. We then ran into a strong gale from the east that brought poor visibility, including sleet and heavy snow. Even the Greenland men were concerned about our condition. There was no sight of land; there was no Terra Australis.

We headed for New Zealand, and the only casualties to scurvy were a few sheep; not a man was seriously sick, nor had been. The *Adventure* had been on its own for some time, and when we reconnected, I was shocked by what I saw. Scurvy was rampant aboard the ship—even though proper foods had been abundantly available. I immediately ordered daily consumption of celery, fresh fish, fresh foods boiled with wheat or oatmeal, and soups. The men, being properly looked after, soon recovered, but we had lost a month.

We set sail eastward to look once more for a sign of Terra Australis. Once again we found ourselves in wild westerly gales, howling in the rigging and bringing up a vicious wintry sea smashing at the rudder, violently throwing the helmsman over the wheel. Had the office of the watch not immediately jumped to the wheel and held the spokes, the rudder, banging wildly, might have destroyed itself.

We'd been at sea less than a month and were headed to Tahiti. The *Adventure* already had twenty cases of scurvy. The *Resolution* had none. The *Adventure* captain had been doing his best, but my dietary method wasn't enough. All my methods had to go with it—cleanliness at all times, airing the quarters and the hold with iron pots of charcoal fires, insistence on the consumption of the full issue of anti-scorbutics, unrelenting attention to detail in the care of quarters and men, whether they liked it or not. Murdock, the *Adventure*'s cook, died— being dirtily inclined, there was no possibility of making him keep himself clean. More delays.

With a trip lasting over 1,000 days, I couldn't go into all the details. However, suffice it to say scurvy was increasing on the *Adventure*. We had to send fit men from our ship to fill in for their sick men. At one point they lost a boat's crew, killed and eaten by the Maori. While in Matavai Bay, we rested for a few weeks, but left due to political problems. Next, we arrived at the Society Islands, where thievery was almost a sport. We continued to endure strong gales with thick fog, sleet, and snow at times. The picture to be painted is one where there were constant obstacles and situations to work through. We did work through them and make it home.

Though all my goals were not met, the problems in illness and navigation we experienced formed a basis for the discovery of Australia and the conquering of scurvy. I lost only one man out of 118 in more than 1,000 days; I had conquered scurvy.

Take care of the people around you, look after their needs, sympathize with them. They will serve you well and be healthier workers, mentally and physically. I pray that I will be remembered for the example and standards that I set in sea travel. With the threat of scurvy being dissolved, there were fewer barriers against making the long trips to the beautiful Pacific.

I must tell you my death was far too premature; there was still much to be done. I loved the Pacific and felt I was perhaps a protector of her lands. For you see, I believe I knew the new Australia and the young New Zealand better than anyone else on earth. I had only scratched the surface of these wonderful frontiers. I might have helped to get both countries started more effectively and keep a useful and benevolent eye on Tahiti and the Hawaiian and Friendly Islands as well.

Sincerely,

Captain James Cook

Thomas Edison

"INVENTOR"

*...responsible for developing
the electric light bulb. Among his other
successes were an electric generating
system, a sound recording device, and
the motion picture projector.*

1847–1931

Thomas Alva Edison, generally recognized as the most prolific inventor in history, came from a poor Midwestern background and gave little evidence early on that he would someday be regarded as "The Wizard of Menlo Park." Edison patented 1,093 inventions. Although his favorite was the phonograph (No one had ever before recorded the sound of a human voice), his most famous was the electric light. His invention of the electric light bulb—wondrous in itself—was exceeded only by Edison's success in making it available to millions, thanks to his ability to design the world's first electric-power stations. Because of his work during World War I, when he served as president of the Naval Consulting Board and did research on torpedo mechanisms, Edison was awarded the Distinguished Service medal. Edison's tenacity was unparalleled. Once, while working with a storage battery—and failing to get the results he wanted after about 10,000 tries—he was consoled by a friend. Edison's reply? "Why, I have not failed. I've just found 10,000 ways that won't work."

THOMAS EDISON

Mr. Andy Andrews
P.O. Box 2761
Gulf Shores, Alabama 36547

Dear Andy Andrews,

Though I am, my dear fellow, honored by your request for some insight into the human drama that accompanies one's journey through the great storms of his life, I must caution that because of my seeming peculiar nature, this letter will be brief.

For more than a year now, I have been laboring on yet another invention—a labor that has me closeted in my Menlo Park compound here in New Jersey—and I haven't time to sleep, much less ponder the vicissitudes of life. I do maintain, however, that what I have described as peculiar, or what others have described as eccentric, about my behavior is exactly what has enabled me to patent hundreds of inventions (my favorite being the phonograph): I work, and work some more, and work longer still. For though I am not a classically educated man, I am far better off than the man who is university molded, but who does not comprehend the benefits of long hours and intrepid spirit. I have found that it is fortitude, not classroom education, that is changing the world for the better. As I have said before, there is no substitute for hard work—genius is one percent inspiration and 99 percent perspiration.

My efforts now are wholly concentrated on finding an electric light that will be made useful to the common man in his everyday affairs, one that will last for hours on end and enable whole towns and cities to carry out their affairs at nighttime as well as in daylight. Thus far, I have met with failure after failure; and with each failure, I am even more certain that my team of workers and I will soon see the light, so to speak.

In a nutshell, Andy, that process which I've just described in this letter is the secret to success. It is failure! Let me digress for a moment.

When I was eight years old, my parents moved the family from Milan, Ohio, to Port Huron, Michigan. Not used to the colder weather, I came down with scarlet fever. As a result, my entrance into grammar school was delayed until I was nearly nine. As far as I was concerned, that delay should have been indefinite, for I found nothing more repulsive than being forced to sit for hours in a room and having a mean-spirited minister attempt to pound into my brain information from books, books that I would rather have read myself. I found myself daydreaming constantly, and so did the reverend—who would then get his point across with a leather strap. The day he called me "addled" was the day I ran from the schoolhouse and vowed never to return. My father, I believe, already felt that I was stupid and incorrigible, but my mother, to her credit, confronted the teacher and resolved to teach me at home.

That was not my first confrontation with failure, but probably my most important, because rather than despairing my plight, I flourished under my mother's tutelage and learned much about nature by tinkering with chemicals and doo-dads in the basement. It was at that time that I learned the value of failure and saw that it would always, inevitably, lead to success.

My entire work life, it seems, took that same course; in the years that followed, I was hired and fired too many times to provide an accurate count. I certainly had difficulty with discipline, I concede, and I was astonished that time after time, my employment would be terminated only because my curiosity and desire to discover better, more economical ways to perform a task were not appreciated and seen only as behavior that was contemptuous of authority.

Even as I write this letter, my mind is reeling with the possibilities of a light bulb that a person can switch on and off at his pleasure. Wouldn't that be nice?

Even nicer, I'll admit, is the adulation of those who believe me to be a wizard of sorts (They're calling me the "Wizard of Menlo Park"). I can't tell you how much more important that is to me than all the money I've been told I'll earn once we get this light bulb perfected. For I don't care so much about making my fortune as I do for getting ahead of the other fellows, many of whom have ideas, but little desire to embellish them, save for financial reward.

With this current project, I have run into tremendous obstacles, from lack of money (though, finally, my agent has procured the promise of a sizable advance from Western Union) to the problem of motivating my team to push as hard as I do. I am forever urging these men to remember that nothing that's good works by itself, just to please you; you've got to *make* the darn thing work.

I must close now, Andy. I only hope that your readers can take heart during those many days of self-doubt that are sure to lie ahead, that they must not let the failures get them down. They must remember that it is only because of those failures that they will eventually come out ahead and be better individuals in the end.

My best regards,

Thomas A. Edison

"Nothing external has
any power over you."

Ralph Waldo Emerson

William Penn

"FOUNDER"

*...was the founder of
the colony of Pennsylvania.
He was the son of
Admiral William Penn.*

1644–1718

Philadelphia is well known as the City of Brotherly Love. The city was conceived and so christened in the mind of William Penn years before a suitable location was found to build it on. Penn was a well-educated young man and the son of a social war hero, the admiral Sir William Penn, in seventeenth-century England. It was a tumultuous political time, not long after Cromwell had defeated the Crown in a civil war. The victory was short-lived, and after twenty years, the Crown was reestablished. At that time, any other opinion differing from the royal-mandated religion was not tolerated. Nonconformity meant certain imprisonment and sometimes a death sentence.

Penn was a Quaker, a religious zealot in defiance of the Crown's forced religious subjugation. He spent many years in the prisons of London, where he wrote famous books in defense of religious tolerance. This partly led to his liberation.

As a debt due to his late father, Penn was awarded a large land mass in America. He called it Pennsylvania, and there he carried out his "Holy Experiment." Penn established a territory where all men were equal. His brother Quakers inhabited the land and lived peaceably among the Native Americans. William Penn wrote of his tremendous admiration and respect for the Indians. He dealt fairly with them, instead of taking lands from them, as was his legal right of conquer. He purchased everything at a fair price.

Penn's political imagination furnished Jefferson and the later framers of the Constitution with a bold and persuasive precedent for democracy in America. His personality and values marked the American venture at its very outset with traits that have since shaped America's self-image as well as her basic conflicts: politics as the expression of moral concern, and defiance of authority in the name of justice.

WILLIAM PENN

Mr. Andy Andrews
P.O. Box 2761
Gulf Shores, Alabama 36547

Dear Mr. Andrews,

Great accomplishments are never achieved without great cost. I was a man of staunch political and religious principles. The uncompromising philosophy I adhered to cost me many years of my life spent in prison, social disgrace, a broken relationship with my father, and at times a faltering of my very hope. Nevertheless, though the pain and distress of these trials, at the time, seemed unbearable, I now would not change these courses of events. For I was able, through the trials of such adversity, to become strong and rise to challenges I would not otherwise have been able to bear.

I grew up in the shadow of a giant. My father, William Penn Sr., was a famous naval officer who had victoriously fought many brave sea battles for England. Over the years, he became a hero and social idol, a great figure of national pride. He was an exceedingly wealthy man. My father was loyal to the Crown and to the Anglican religion of England. When Cromwell was victorious over King Charles, my father remained faithful to the Crown in his heart, although he was retained as a high naval officer in the revolutionary navy during its upheaval of the monarchy. During this time, I was a teen and attending school at Oxford. It was there that I came to form my own perceptions of right and wrong and of religious conviction. My religious beliefs did not run parallel with my father's. I became a Quaker, one who believes in the personal relationship with God and holds that all men are created equal under the God that created us.

I was soon forced to face the consequences of dissension. I was arrested with a group of other Quakers. The judge knew that I was the son of a nobleman and did not believe that I could be a Quaker. He imprisoned the others, but released me. I then walked to the bench and declared myself a Quaker and asked to be charged with the same criminal offense as my comrades. He obliged and wrote to my father about the matter. My father rebuked me and attempted to shame me. The conflict between the military hero and his pacifist son became something of a national embarrassment. I saw only that my father desired me as an ornament to his already gloriously adorned reputation. I did not feel he respected me for what I truly believed. I went back to Oxford and was soon again imprisoned for my beliefs.

My father disowned me for my disloyalty and criminal behavior. He felt I had betrayed him. My father was also my hero, but this was now a ruined relationship. I felt compelled to search for something deeper than mere wealth and public adulation. Yet again I went to prison for my nonconformity to the Crown's political and religious mandates. During this time, I was plagued with self-doubt. I was tortured not only by the barbarous prison keepers, but by my own heart, which condemned me when I thought of my father. Nevertheless, I could not forsake what I was spiritually convinced of. The intersection of politics and religion is inescapable, and unless dealt with in godly wisdom, only erects an edifice for the purpose of a tremendous fall.

At the age of twenty-four I had resolved to put my knowledge of theology and my legal learning at the service of my religion. Through the power of print, I would become the Quakers' spokesman and defender. I had lost my claim to an honorable inheritance or any good graces with the newly restored royalty of King Charles II, who had come to power largely due to my father's efforts. Socially, I was a disgrace. But I had courage. I had learning; I had a banner to carry and I had the good grace of God to help me. I put aside my self-doubt. I determined to face the adventure that came to me in pursuit of the truth.

I defended myself and another Quaker in court after being arrested for publicly declaring our faith. I was successful. So successful, in fact, that the judge became enraged and threatened to kill the jurors unless they changed their verdict to guilty. They also had courage. Although themselves imprisoned for finding me not guilty, they would not change their verdict. An appeals court freed us all, and a test case set the precedent that a judge could not compel a jury to find a specific verdict against their own conscience. I was freed from prison.

I had the good fortune of generating my own notoriety by my own merits. I became respected even by some who did not hold my personal beliefs as their own. I was also able to reconcile with my father while he was upon his deathbed. Over the many years of estrangement, we somehow had forged a mutual respect for one another. My father's last action was to ensure with the King's brother that I would enjoy the goodwill and protection of the Crown. This ironically cast me in a dual role: I would be counselor to the King, while at the same time, serving as leader of the dissident Quakers. This dual role eventually culminated in my greatest achievement: the founding of Pennsylvania.

I inherited my father's fortune and employed a fellow Quaker, John Ford, to oversee my financial affairs. I received an American colony from the Crown as payment of a debt to my father. Unwanted by my own countrymen, I used this storm of perfection to the advantage of a higher purpose. I decided to establish a land of social and political equality. It would be a place ruled by the will of the people, with the opportunity for all to seek their own happiness in life, including the choice of their own religion. Immediately, many of the English Quakers crossed the great Atlantic to establish a new life in this "Holy Experiment" of political and religious freedom. Before there were enough settlers there to populate a small town, I had staked out the position for a great metropolis I would call Philadelphia. I met with the Native Americans and dealt generously with them. I found that they already worshiped a great spirit, and it was not difficult to correlate this with the one and true God. They were a friendly, ingenious, and generous people.

I governed Pennsylvania for two years, until I needed to come to the aid of my fellow Quakers in England. Those two years had changed the face of England. It was now ruled by King William and Queen Mary. They were suspicious of me as a dissenter of religious beliefs and brought charges of treason against me. I hid in ghettos and the street for four long years in an attempt to keep my freedom and my life. Ultimately, the charges were rescinded.

I returned to my beloved Pennsylvania. I then found out that my financial overseer and fellow Quaker, John Ford, had cheated me. I was in financial ruin. Although his death precipitated this discovery, his wife had filed court actions against me, claiming that Pennsylvania belonged to her, and that I owed her a great sum of money. Would my torments ever end? Her documents were falsified, but nevertheless, I was forced again to return to England, where my colony was restored to me. But I was found to owe her the money she claimed, on the basis of her falsified documents. I went to debtors' prison at the age of sixty-two. My Quaker brethren lent me the money to get out of prison. I then spent the duration of my days in England with my wife and children.

My life would not have been directed in the proper path had these storms not blown upon my horizon. I would not have had the occasion to write the "Frame of Government," which contained my philosophy of government for Pennsylvania a century before the founding of the United States. I was able to pioneer a libertarian republic at the edge of the wilderness and set up new institutional models for man's most fundamental relations: to God and to state. I met my calling and rose to my challenges because of the storms I was made to endure.

Best regards to all,

William Penn

"You never achieve real success
unless you like what you're doing."

Dale Carnegie

Mark Twain

"AUTHOR/ HUMORIST"

*…is considered to be the greatest
American humorist.
He was equally successful in writing for
children and adults.*

1835–1910

Samuel Langhorne Clemens, better known to the world as Mark Twain, was one of America's best-loved authors. Twain was one of those rare authors who could draw his readers right into a story. When he tells of the mighty Mississippi, you suddenly find yourself floating down the river.

He grew up in Hannibal, Missouri, a Mississippi river port, which gave him the setting for his two most celebrated books: *The Adventures of Tom Sawyer* (1876) and *The Adventures of Huckleberry Finn* (1884).

In all, Twain wrote twenty-three books. His writing has been praised for its realism of place and language, memorable characters, and hatred of hypocrisy and oppression. A few of Twain's own favorites were *The Prince and the Pauper* (1882), a children's book; *A Connecticut Yankee in King Arthur's Court* (1889); and *Personal Recollections of Joan of Arc* (1896), a sentimental biography.

Twain became quite a celebrity, frequently speaking out on public issues. He was recognized as the man in the white linen suit, which he always wore when making public appearances.

Twain attended a log cabin school until he was twelve. That was the only formal education he had; yet Yale and Oxford universities gave him honorary degrees, and his companionship was sought by the most learned men on earth. He claimed a diploma from the school of hard knocks.

Mark Twain

Mr. Andy Andrews
P.O. Box 2761
Gulf Shores, Alabama 36547

Dear Sir,

My lifelong dream, since I was a boy, had always been to succeed as a writer. In fact, most people only knew me as a literary figure. If I do say so myself, I did have the ability to put pen to paper and create a thrilling adventure.

Problem was . . . I hated it. Now, let me explain. I didn't hate being a writer or having written or the money that came with it. I just got aggravated with the process. Sitting down to a blank piece of paper can get old!

So, I decided to take the money I had made and invest it. I would make money that did not depend on my creating something out of nothing. Unfortunately, my business sense being what it was, I quickly did just that—turned something into nothing!

I invested in a steam generator that wouldn't generate. I invested in a watch company that didn't tick long enough to pay its first dividend. I invested in a steam pulley that never pulled. I started a publishing company that failed and invested heavily in a machine that was supposed to typeset. The only thing it set was *me*. It set me back a pretty penny.

Then one day I met a man named Alexander Graham Bell. Bell tried to persuade me to invest my money in a new machine he had invented. He told me I would be able to talk on this machine to someone who might be more than five blocks away. Absurd! I might've been a fool, but I wasn't an idiot. I passed.

Needless to say, at age fifty-eight, I found myself overwhelmed by debt. Certainly, it would have been easy to bypass my obligations through bankruptcy, but I didn't. I resolved to pay back every cent I owed. There was only one way I knew that I could do this, and that was by writing. So, write I did.

I suppose those business failures were a road back to pen and paper. I might never have written another book had I not been forced to financially. It is said that pressure creates diamonds. I know for a fact that financial pressure squeezed a book out of me. *A Connecticut Yankee in King Arthur's Court* was the first one.

Many more followed. Not necessarily because I had to have the money, but because I didn't want to part with my original dream. I wanted to succeed as a writer. The work, I had to remember, was what made the success worthwhile.

Don't part with your dreams. When you give them up, you may still exist, but you will have ceased to live.

Sincerely,

S.L. Clemens
Mark Twain

Mark Twain

"Let no man be deluded that a
knowledge of the path can
substitute for putting
one foot in front of the other."

Mary Caroline Richards

Benjamin Franklin

"STATESMAN/ PRINTER/ INVENTOR"

...helped draft the Declaration of Independence. His contributions to the cause of the American Revolution rank him among the country's greatest statesmen.

1706–1790

Ben Franklin is perhaps the greatest statesman this country has ever produced. He was a man of incredible abilities in a largely diverse scope of disciplines. He was a foreign diplomat for America during the Revolutionary War—a philosopher, writer, scientist, and inventor. The rocking chair, the wood burning stove, and bifocal glasses were all contributions of Benjamin Franklin. He continues to be such a presence in our lives today that it is no wonder he was chosen to appear on the $100 dollar bill. Except for Susan B. Anthony, he is the only person depicted on American currency who did not serve as president.

To learn of Benjamin Franklin's life is to examine an incredibly successful man, but most have never heard about the challenges he faced or the disasters that befell him prior to his becoming an enduring national hero. Franklin's life, however successful and gloriously portrayed in most history books, was ridden with misfortune and disappointment. Though Franklin's accomplishments were many, and cannot be understated, perhaps his greatest achievement was found in his ability to pull himself up by his bootstraps and press on after being set back and knocked down so many times.

Benjamin Franklin
Pennsylvania Abolition Society

Andy Andrews
P.O. Box 2761
Gulf Shores, Alabama 36547

Dear Andy,

I was flattered to receive your request to contribute to your book. I trust that by revealing some of the difficulties I have endured and overcome, others will be inspired to conquer their own hardships by focusing on their dreams.

My father, Josiah, a destitute immigrant, sailed to the New World from England in 1683. He was a decidedly religious man, and although very poor, held fast to his Christian virtues. He believed only hard, honest work brought reward. My father earned a meager income as a tallow chandler in the colonial settlement of Boston. From the wages he earned, he supported his wife and eleven children. Consequently, there was little of anything to spare, and I grew up appreciating the smallest of possessions.

I was the seventh child of my father's second wife; his first wife died in childbirth. I was the youngest of the eleven surviving children. My father had decided early that I was to become a minister; this was the family's tithe to the church. Even as a young boy, I loved to learn and to read books. My father enrolled me in a school to learn Latin. I quickly rose to the top of my class and was scheduled to be advanced a full grade due to my aptitude for learning.

My intent in life while enrolled in this school was to pass into Harvard, the next step along the path of theological progress in Boston of those days. I never was advanced that grade, however. In fact, I was removed from the school altogether. Having so large a family, my father could not afford to continue my education for the ministry. My first career pursuit was a failure.

I therefore was tutored in writing and arithmetic. The years of learning were to be followed by apprenticeship to my father. As a tallow chandler's apprentice, I was employed in the most menial of tasks: cutting wicks for candles, filling the dipping mold and molds for cast candles, attending the shop, going on errands, etc. It was a miserable existence in many ways. Although I was young, my future appeared dismal, fated to a life of mediocrity.

At the age of twelve I was apprenticed to my older brother, James, who was a printer in Boston. I had long since developed a love for books, and found I enjoyed printing them as much as reading them. Although I was a menial laborer, I put my heart into it and fully loved my work. I had access to books, which I devoured regularly. This trained me to present arguments in a diplomatic fashion. In order to boost my brother's sales in a competitive printer's market, I began to write verses and ballads. I was highly criticized by my father for this. He strongly discouraged my budding writing ability and shamed my attempts at it. Nevertheless, the venture was an economic success for my brother.

Unfortunately, my brother blackballed me from pursuing a printing profession anywhere I went in Boston. It seemed as though I had been overcome by yet another failure.

So, at sixteen years of age, I ran away, seeking whatever I could find in the vast expanse of the New World. I smuggled myself aboard ships and traveled also by boat to New York, New Jersey, and Delaware. I went hungry. I had little money. I became a weary vagabond, a youth beginning to wish I had never left home. I found myself in Philadelphia, where the governor of Pennsylvania himself deluded me into believing he would establish me as his personal printer if I would only go to England to acquire the equipment and bring it back at his expense. I was sailing East, far into the Atlantic Ocean, when I discovered I was a victim of a ruthless prank.

Upon my return from England, I devised a plan to apply myself industriously to whatever business I took in hand, and not divert my mind from my business by any foolish prospect for growing suddenly rich; for industry and patience are the surest means of plenty. I eventually prevailed in establishing my own printing business in Philadelphia. I became successful in this endeavor, which opened the doors to many favorable opportunities.

I attained success, wealth, and notoriety. I established relationships with foreign dignitaries, which helped me to solicit and secure French support in the American Revolutionary War. I discovered a love for science and experimentation, at a time when scientific investigation was equivalent to blasphemy. But with persistence, I discovered and devised many helpful inventions from my scientific exploits, ultimately overcoming social objections, which were based on ignorance. I had come to realize that tenacity would ultimately prevail over resistance and obstacles of whatever nature, and in prevailing over them, many wonderful accomplishments awaited.

History would go on to record me as "A boy who walked the streets of Philadelphia, munching on a loaf of bread, a youth who rose from a printer's apprentice to become the new world's first great publisher, the man who invented stoves for his compatriot's warmth, and designed lightning rods for their safety, the executive who gathered supplies for Braddock's march into the wilderness, the sage who signed himself "Poor Richard," the diplomat who raised a loan in France to gain his country's freedom, the patriot who shared in framing the Declaration of Independence, the Constitution, and the treaties with Britain and France, a man unsurpassed in the range of his natural gifts and to the important uses he put them to."

I have basked in the good fortune of having attained the respect and praise of many ingenious and worthy men over several generations. I have been blessed by the Good Lord to have left a legacy such as few people are able to memorialize. But though it may seem to many that I possessed some unique, innate talent to succeed, my noted achievements came by virtue of drawing from a common endowment the Lord has placed in every human spirit, though so infrequently employed. . . Persistence!

Indeed, Andy, it was my resolve and stamina which catalyzed my success. And I am persuaded that it is not so only as these qualities pertained to me, but that they comprise a general principle which applies to everyone: Persistence is a requisite of success and utility. And I would rather have it said of me, "He lived usefully" than "He died rich."

My Warmest Regards,

Benjamin Franklin

Ulysses S. Grant

"MILITARY LEADER/ PRESIDENT"

... was the Union Army's greatest general. He led his troops to victory in the Civil War and later served two terms as president.

1822–1885

U.S. Grant was the son of an Ohio tanner. He grew up without a strong self-image, and mainly due to his father's ambition, not his own, attended West Point. He graduated in the middle of his class. He served under General Zachary Taylor in the Mexican War, where he was not particularly well thought of. In all, Grant lived a life of circumstance, allowing the happenings around him to shape his destiny rather than creating his own future. U.S. Grant began his adult life and military career as a very passive personality.

At the outbreak of the Civil War, he was working at his father's leather store in Galena, Illinois. He joined the military to help his family financially and was appointed by the governor to command a regiment of unruly volunteers. He created a fighting unit from the band and rose to the rank of brigadier general of volunteers. From there, Grant's military career took shape, leading President Lincoln to defend him against his detractors, saying, "I can't spare this man, he fights!" Finally, at a courthouse in Appomattox, Virginia, he accepted the unconditional surrender of General Robert E. Lee. This single event, along with the way it was handled by Grant, paved a smooth road to the White House. U.S. Grant died shortly after finishing his memoirs in 1885.

ULYSSES S. GRANT

Mr. Andy Andrews
P.O. Box 2761
Gulf Shores, Alabama 36547

Dear Andy,

Where do I begin? Reviewing a life divided into halves with surgical precision, one half representing profound failure and the other profound success, I am hard pressed to find an element of reason to make any sense of it all.

Was it the Civil War? This great conflict certainly marks my life's division, but did it create the difference in U.S. Grant? I cannot say.

Was it my upbringing? My parents were good to us. My father stood by me even in times it seemed the town we lived in held my shortcomings as the one thing they could all agree upon. But was it his love that catapulted me into the highest office in the land? I cannot say.

Or was it an undying fighting spirit that had me meeting challenge after challenge with my chin held high? Absolutely not! I was never known for, nor did I possess, this strength of personality.

I believe if I look honestly and fairly at my curious life, I would come to the conclusion that Divine Providence played the starring role, not U.S. Grant at all. Allow me to elaborate.

I was born at Point Pleasant, Ohio, on April 27, 1822, to wonderful parents, Hanna Simpson and Jesse Grant. My father owned a tannery and was an aggressive, verbose man, yet loving and supportive.

I recall his advice prior to my first attempt at horse trading. I was eight years old. Though the asking price was $25, my father had instructed me to offer less. Excited, I ran to my first economic battle and openly stated, "My father told me to offer you $20, and if you don't agree, I am to offer you $22, and if you still don't agree, I am to give you $25." The news of my horse-trading ability spread through town quickly, and I became the butt of continual joking and barbed sneers. The feeling in town was that I was a stupid, slothful boy. This perception may have fought its way out of this situation. However, I chose to draw within, remain alone, and wait for opportunity to pass within reach. Then I would seize it and hold on with great tenacity.

The first of these unlikely opportunities occurred when my father, always wanting the best for me, heard that a friend's son had been dismissed from West Point. He immediately wrote his congressman to apply for the position on my behalf before news of the opening spread. The congressman received the letter (the only application to that point) the day before his term expired. Anxious to do a favor for a constituent, the congressman signed the letter approving the appointment without checking my credentials. In his haste, he also made a mistake in my name, endowing me with my mother's maiden name, Simpson, as my middle name. And this is how I came to have the significant initials of U.S. Perhaps this was an omen!

I graduated from West Point twenty-first in a class of thirty-nine, and though I requested appointment to the dragoons, I received orders as brevet second lieutenant in the Fourth Regiment of Infantry. I felt it was a tribute to my mediocrity. Still, I had seized something many had not.

In the years following, I was assigned to one lonely, out-of-the-way post after another. And, though a wonderful young lady accepted my proposal of marriage just before I rode off to the Mexican-American War, I continued to fall into depressed spirits and low self-esteem.

In that state, I began drinking too often and too much. In fact, when reprimanded about this, I chose to resign my position rather than have my new wife, Julia Dent, discover that I was called for such an offense. I rode home in despair. My ineptitude followed me into my business life, where failure seemed almost certain and indeed met me there. I will never forget one of my darkest memories. Christmas eve 1858, poverty found me pawning my watch in order to bring cheer to my family, which at that time numbered four. I was far too preoccupied with the immediate task of feeding my family to follow the affairs of state during those dark days. However, the turmoil of our nation set the wheels of change in motion and turned a favorable eye toward U.S. Grant. For when my old unit departed for the state capital to be mustered into service, I was in need of gainful employment and so joined them. Thus began my journey to Appomattox, the White House, and fame.

How could over forty years of failure mysteriously become such incredible success? As I stated before, Divine Providence. Divine Providence and a quiet, ever watchful eye ready to seize even the smallest spark of opportunity and fan it into a flame.

My critics called me lucky, my friends called me a quiet genius. I believe neither. I simply leave you with this thought. No matter your situation or circumstances, keep your eyes open and your heart of hearts expectant. Then, when true opportunity passes near, seize it with your heart and hold it there. Against all odds, hold it tight and make it yours. Then all things are possible, even the highest office in the land!

Sincerely,

U.S. Grant

Florence Nightingale

"HUMANITARIAN"

...founded the Nightingale Home and School for Nurses. She made invaluable contributions to the evolution of nursing as a profession.

1820–1910

Although she was born into wealth and could have lived a life of idleness, Florence Nightingale chose to work all of her life. And what wonderful work she did: from childhood she had wanted to be a nurse, but had to fight for the right to become one.

Not only did she become a nurse, but a teacher of nurses, establishing the first and foremost school of nurses' training in London. Because of her efforts, nursing became a well-respected profession. Nightingale was also a brilliant administrator: She ran hospitals and was one of the first to establish the need for hygienic procedures in hospitals. Her later writings became textbooks for nurses and were translated into many languages.

In 1907 she became the first woman to receive the British Order of Merit, as well as many honors from foreign governments. She also realized that her work was to be part of the new women's movement, which was just beginning in the mid-1800s.

Florence Nightingale

Nightingale School and Home for Nurses
London, England

Mr. Andy Andrews
P.O. Box 2761
Gulf Shores, Alabama 36547

Dear Mr. Andrews,

I welcome the opportunity to have contact with you, because although many people know of my accomplishments in the field of nursing, few know the hurdles I had to overcome to even be permitted to become a nurse!

I was born into a wealthy English family and could have lived a life of leisure. But I burned to work, to be useful at something. I felt as if all my being was gradually drawing to one point. That thing was nursing. It was my calling.

However, there were moral and social objections. Gentlewomen like me, it was felt, would be exposed to moral dangers if they entered nursing. At that time, only lower-class women became nurses, and the profession itself was held in low esteem. Nurses were noted for moral excesses such as drinking on the job—and worse.

But finally, my persistence paid off. I was permitted to enter nurses' training, and I directed all my intellectual and emotional fervor to achieving my goals of becoming a good nurse. I ultimately became superintendent of the Hospital for Invalid Gentlewomen in London.

It was at about that time that the importance of sanitation became known as a vital factor in healing the sick and preventing the spread of disease in hospital wards. Heretofore, people often died in hospitals because sterile conditions were not practiced.

I took my knowledge with me when I worked at a British barracks hospital during the Crimean War. Through my efforts, the mortality rate among the sick and wounded was greatly reduced. As a matter of fact, as a result of my reforms, the number of English soldiers who died was reduced to half that of prior years.

Although my accomplishments were highly regarded in many circles, there was strife, including turmoil in the religious arena. At one time, both Catholics and Protestants attacked my efforts. However, an Irish clergyman, when asked to what sect I belonged, replied, "She belongs to a sect which, unfortunately, is a very rare one—the sect of the Good Samaritan." In any case, I finally weathered that storm. Perhaps it was my outspokenness that aroused concern. For I never failed to say exactly what I thought.

I was able to found the Nightingale School and Home for Nurses in London. This marked the beginning of professional education in nursing. In other words, here were sown the seeds for the present-day practice of nursing, which has come to be a respected profession, with its highly skilled practitioners taking great responsibility alongside doctors.

Although I suffered ill health myself, I never stopped working. I became particularly interested in the question of hospital construction and wrote several papers on this subject, papers which became the germ for my rather famous *Notes on Hospitals*. My writings on hospital procedures and my observations on sanitary conditions in army hospitals and barracks were greatly studied and were put to good use. As a result, the Barracks and Hospitals Improvement Commission was established: Buildings now were ventilated and warmed, water supplies improved, kitchens were remodeled, sanitary conditions were established.

Through my urging, hygiene became the key word and formed the most important branch of a young medical officer's instruction. It was I who pressed for the introduction of female nurses into the army, and with the benefit of good training, they represented the most highly trained and professional element in army medical circles.

I am amazed to see some of my ideas still in practice today. These ideas might have been discovered years later (or not at all) had I not persisted in my chosen profession. There were those who discouraged me and some who tried to stop me altogether. If you persist, you will always win—and win your critics over!

I am, yours, most cordially,

Florence Nightingale

Florence Nightingale

"I hear and I forget.
I see and I remember.
I do and I understand."

Chinese Proverb

John Hancock

"PATRIOT/ STATESMAN"

*...first man to
sign the Declaration of Independence.
He was the first governor of the State of
Massachusetts.*

1737–1793

John Hancock's signature is the most prominently penned name upon the United States' Declaration of Independence. After signing his name in such a manner, he later said that he had written his name so boldly because he wanted the British to make no mistake about how he felt. John Hancock was a man driven by a purpose of destiny and equity. Hancock was one of the foremost American patriots of the Revolutionary War. His presence was critical to the attitude and morale of our soldiers.

John Hancock was thirty-nine years old when he signed his name at the bottom of that historic document. He would live to see his purpose and destiny a reality. John Hancock's story was not particularly unique to the turbulent times preceding the American Revolution. What was unique was the way he took circumstances framing his life, and used those circumstances to fuel his resolve and make his society a better one. He went on to become the first governor of the State of Massachusetts, and was holding that position at the time of his death.

J O H N   H A N C O C K

Mr. Andy Andrews
P.O. Box 2761
Gulf Shores, Alabama 36547

Dear Sir,

I came into this world on January 23, 1737, on the coldest day Quincy, Massachusetts, had seen that year. A warm family, however, welcomed me to life. My father and his brothers were of an entrepreneurial bent and were, for that time, quite successful.

After graduating from Harvard in 1754, I joined the mercantile firm of my uncle, Thomas. In 1764, I inherited the family enterprise and a small fortune. Most of that fortune was wrapped up in a trading ship. We called her *Liberty*.

Soon, I was elected to the Massachusetts legislature. I was a man of substantial financial posture at that time, and with the political influence added to my life, the future seemed bright indeed. Then, almost without warning, a storm hit.

My quartermaster on the *Liberty* refused to pay excessive additional import duties on a shipment of Madeira wine. The British then seized my ship. They took my property, my livelihood, and my inheritance. The harsh move of a government against an individual changed the course of history.

My refusal to roll over and die brought many to my side. I vigorously defended myself in courts, and although my lawsuits were in vain, I won wide popularity with the anti-British element in Boston.

After British troops fired on unarmed men protesting taxation without representation in 1770, I served on a committee demanding their removal from Boston. Soon, I was prominently identified with the colonial cause and became a leader of the Whig, or Patriot, Party in Massachusetts. After the Battles of Lexington and Concord, which began our revolution, I was specifically excluded from the general amnesty offered to revolutionary leaders by the British.

The story of war and our subsequent victory is today a part of common knowledge. The catalyst of the upheaval is, of

course, less well known. It is important to note that I was not
the only person who had a ship stolen by the government.
Mine was not the only inheritance lost. I was at the time, however, the only person who decided to take a bad situation and
let it engineer a change in the future.

Was my action risky? Yes. Were the results worth it? You be
the judge. Today you only hear about the revolution itself or
the 200 years of freedom you have enjoyed. As I put my "John
Hancock" on the first line of the Declaration of Independence, I
knew it had all come about because of the worst time in my life.

Sincerely,

John Hancock

"Where there is no vision,
the people perish..."

Proverbs 29:18

Pablo Picasso

"ARTIST"

*...considered to be the
founder of the Cubist movement in art.
During his lifetime, he created more
than 20,000 works.*

1881–1973

Pablo Picasso is universally considered the greatest artist of the twentieth century. He was primarily a painter, but was also considered a master in the art of sculpture, engravings, and ceramics. Picasso is perhaps best remembered for his "blue" and "rose" periods of painting, where he used these hues as the dominant color schemes in his paintings. Subsequently, Picasso opened the gateway to Cubism and modern abstract art through a variety of paintings, sculptures, and drawings.

While it is sometimes unclear as to just what meaning a painter may have intended to reveal in a particular work, there is much more to art than merely a picture contained in a framework of wood. Picasso himself once said that he only painted what his mind's eye saw, and left it to others to interpret what it should mean. Curiously, the master himself thought his artwork spoke for itself and felt it silly that people should attempt to interpret it at all. In his letter, Picasso uses words to paint a self-portrait of trial, distress, hunger, and ultimately his own prevailing spirit.

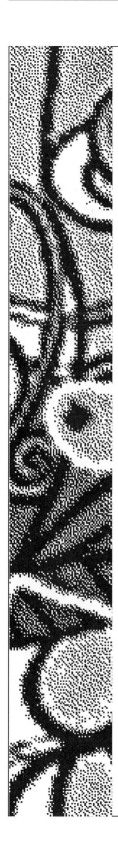

PABLO PICASSO

Mr. Andy Andrews
P.O. Box 2761
Gulf Shores, Alabama 36547

Dear Mr. Andrews,

My aptitude for artistic ability was recognized by
my father at a very young age. He was a painter
himself, and taught at an art school in my homeland
of Spain. My father continually supported my artistic future. But had I known as a child the many
years of hardship I was destined to face as an
artist, I may have never sat before a canvas. By the
time I was fifteen, I had already mastered realistic
technique and the ability to paint true-life images. I
could paint quickly and finish three paintings in the
time it took most to complete one. I met with a
modest amount of adolescent success as a painter,
but I soon became bored with the prospect.

Art traditionally follows closely the literature, architec-
ture, and music of the day. At this time, near the
turn of the century, all of these disciplines displayed
a very structured, fluid, identifiable meter and pre-
dictable pattern. The social philosophy at the time
dictated that a clearly painted image, and one's
ability to create the most realistically painted portrayal, was the hallmark of the finest artist. My philosophy differed, and was to become my first notable
point of nonconformity as an artist. I wanted my art
to be something more.

I felt that I had a talent for art, and that the social
expectations upon artists of the day were shackling
my originality. I began to expand my drawings and
paintings to include images of a less discernible
quality. I was only in the infant stages of expressing

my style, and already I came under a barrage of attacks from fellow artists, friends, and even family members for deviating from the social structures and unwritten laws one must faithfully adhere to in a civilized Spanish community. But I could not allow my originality to be quashed. I decided to move to Paris in order to escape a closed-minded society, and to broaden my artistic horizons.

My father, who was poor, provided me with a little money. I had barely enough money to keep me from starving to death; certainly no more. From then on, I knew the meaning of privation and at times the threat of real starvation. I was able to meet new friends, however, many in the same financial straits as I had found myself. Our mutual hardships forged strong relationships as we encouraged many another as artists. I truly revolted from my former artistic constraints and began to let my creativity flow. Although always hungry and broke, I was happy.

Then I fell into a grievous ordeal when I caught scarlet fever. I recovered, but was continually exhausted for a year afterward. I accepted a friend's invitation to live on his farm while recuperating. I was unable to make my own way as an artist, and I could no longer impose upon my friends. Without money or the prospect of artistic success, and in precarious health, I was forced to return home.

I returned with one of my dearest friends, a young man named Carlos Casagems. Carlos had become like a brother to me and was brokenhearted over a newly lost love. My homecoming was painfully disappointing. I faced humiliation and scorn from everyone I had left in Spain. Their self-righteous glares seemed to scream, "We told you so!" I had shirked their folkways to venture out on my own, giving place to my own originality, and failed. I received little or no forgiveness for this sin. I only had Carlos to help me along, but he returned to Paris in a short time. I then received word that Carlos had shot himself upon his return to Paris. I was devastated.

I worked in a small art studio, humbling myself and my artistic abilities to paint realistic portraits for patrons. I continued in this capacity for months, until I was able to save enough money to return to Paris. I could be without friends or money in either place, but at least in Paris I would be free to give rein to my artistic inclinations. I looked up my old friends in Paris. At nineteen years of age, I felt I had already left my youth far behind. I felt I had experienced a full life's measure of sorrow and hardships. But even after my hostile reception in Spain and the death of my friend, much was left to bear.

The changes in my painting did not occur overnight. The breaks with my past, abrupt though they were, occurred in stages; and in this process, each picture seemed like a step forward in a direction which I alone could foresee. The theme of loneliness which was henceforth to dominate my canvas began now to appear in my works. Out of my failures, struggles, loss, and pain in my life, I began what was later coined "The Blue Period" of my artistic career. Even the French art critics found that there was too much soul and not enough form in my paintings.

My works were criticized vehemently. They were described as "odd," in the best of terms, and as the portrayal of the demonic force of attraction of the ugly and the evil, in the more blatant terms. But I had come too far and gone through too much already for their disparaging remarks to stop me. If critics had any effect on me, it was to make me persevere in the path I had chosen and to increase my obstinacy. My contempt for them was my salvation, because it prevented me from making concessions. I grew accustomed to isolation. That was my life.

I developed a pride at a time when everything seemed to conspire to discourage me and to arouse in me legions of self-doubt. One day, those works in which they detected too much soul would be fought for by collectors, but meanwhile, they did not help me to gain material independence.

I was still in dire financial straits. I remained in Paris, but again found myself painting such things as pot-boilers and advertisements for a patent medicine against malfunctioning of the lymphatic glands. From lack of money, I shared a room with a friend, Max Jacob. It was old and in the attic, with only one small window. It had only one bed, so at night, Max slept while I painted, and I slept when he went to work. I was able to get some of my paintings exhibited at art shows, but none sold. I went for days at a time without eating.

I was destitute. There were rare occasions when we were able to cook an omelet, fry some potatoes, or eat some beans. Soon my friend and I became more desperate. My career seemed without a future. I was earning nothing at all; nobody wanted my pictures, and I was living off an already poor friend. One day, my friend and I were both leaning over the balcony of our fifth floor, overlooking the boulevard. The same thought struck us both. But almost immediately I said, "We must not."

Simply to eat, I tried to sell all of my pictures—all of them. Those that had been exhibited, the product of the past few months, my drawings, and my watercolors. All of them for 200 francs. But no one would buy them! It was very cold that winter, and even by piling on all my clothes, I could not keep warm in the drafty room. I was so cold. So, for the sake of a few moments of warmth, I burned all my drawings and watercolors. I saved my paintings and rolled the canvases. I gave them to a friend and again returned to Spain to waste my talent once more.

But soon I returned to Paris and began to take a brighter outlook on life. I began my "Rose Period," using reddish colors and happier themes, which were successful in sales. This generated interest in my previous paintings of the Blue Period, which then became enormously popular. Eventually, I was able to paint what I wanted, any way I wanted. I also moved into other areas of art, including sculpture, engraving, and ceramics. Throughout the remainder of my life, I gave place to my originality. It was not always well received by everyone—particularly my Cubism and abstraction—but I was immensely happy with it.

I became ridiculously wealthy and an artistic legend in my own time. I carried on with my dreams, Mr. Andrews. That is what separated my from many other, less recognized artists. I suggest to your readers they do the same. Thank you for asking for my contribution.

Sincerely,

Pablo Picasso

Pablo Picasso

"Keep away from people who try
to belittle your ambition.
Small people always do that,
but the really great make you feel
that you, too, can become great."

Mark Twain

Henry Ford
"INDUSTRIALIST"

*...best known for his
pioneering achievements in the
automobile industry.*
1863–1947

Good old Yankee ingenuity was the hallmark of Henry Ford. He was an incessant tinkerer and an undaunted dreamer. His mind had always been fixated upon mechanical wizardry. He could not be dissuaded from taking his chosen path, though his discouragements were plentiful. Today's Formula One race cars, the moon buggy, and even modern mobile weaponry have their roots in Ford's humble horseless carriage. By the time Henry Ford died in 1947, his horseless carriage had evolved into a host of gasoline-engine-powered apparatuses that made life easier for people the world over. There have not been many inventors who have had the pleasure of seeing their contributions built upon in such a grandiose fashion within their own lifetimes.

As you read in his letter, Henry Ford faced many obstacles which would have hindered anyone less motivated or less sure of his destiny. The Ford Motor Company, still one of the leading design and engineering dynamos in the automobile industry, carries on with Henry's legacy of determination and excellence. Indeed, Henry Ford developed the first motor vehicle; but more important, he succeeded in the development of his dream.

HENRY FORD
Ford Motor Corporation

Mr. Andy Andrews
P.O. Box 2761
Gulf Shores, Alabama 36547

Dear Andy,

I have always found success to be a matter of correct thinking. I have watched many a man more talented or intellectually gifted than I struggle to make ends meet simply because he continually gave in to the emotional roller coaster. Let me explain.

My father wanted me to become a farmer and ultimately to inherit the family farm, but wind-up toys and anything else with moving parts captured my imagination. This fascination with mechanical items led me to use steam engines for all kinds of farming application.

One day I saw a steam-driven thresher that actually moved under its own power. Now, until that time, threshers and lumber devices were moved from job to job, pulled by horses. This particular steam engine was rotating the wheels by itself. I saw immediately, however, the impracticality of this device.

Since coal supplies were short, the operator had to either carry enough wood to stake the furnace and produce steam or climb down and begin chopping more wood. That day, an idea was born to invent a faster, lighter vehicle run with an efficient fuel—preferably electricity or gasoline.

I began work soon after, but in less than a year, the men who had agreed to back me financially withdrew their support. For several years, I poured every bit of money Clara and I could scrape together into this dream. Finally, I created a working motor. I ran the engine for less than a minute, then put it aside and never cranked it again. The engine worked—that was all I needed to know. A two-cylinder engine was what I was after.

Now understand that until then there were no spark plugs or carburetors. Camshafts, crankshafts, pushrods, piston rings, gears—everything had to be made from scratch. Edsel, my son, was born about that time, and two more sets of financial backers came and went. The consensus seemed to be that I was wasting my time.

Let me interject here how large a part Clara played in our eventual success. I was always certain of the results. They always come if you work hard enough and get the emotional thing under control, but it was a wonderful thing to have a wife who was more confident than I was. If she had doubts, she kept them to herself. She was my "great believer."

For ten more years, we lived in a rented, thirty-one-foot-square house. More financial backers came full of promises and left disgusted. Until one rainy night when, in a neighbor's woodshed, it all came together. My horseless carriage cranked and ran. It wouldn't, however, fit through the door. With an ax and the permission of my neighbor, I finally rode my creation through the side wall of the woodshed out into the rain and all the way to the town square before the engine died. I had done it.

Yes, I had accomplished what I set out to do, but I must point out again that the results were inevitable as long as I continued the work. Therein lies the rub. Most people let their thinking (emotions) dictate their work; therefore, they never gain a consistency or momentum needed for success. Had I only worked during the periods of financial backing, or when Edsel was born, or when my first engine cranked—had I only worked during those periods of euphoria—I would not have gained the consistency or momentum necessary to succeed.

But the results did occur. I continued my daily activity for well over a decade during periods of economic hardship, failed experiments, fickle investors, and yes, even public taunting.

Incidentally, the economic hardships taught me fiscal responsibility. The failed experiments taught me lessons that put us years ahead of the imitators who copied my designs. The fickle investors who couldn't master their emotions or have faith or wait patiently allowed me to own my own product when it was a success. The public taunting taught me humility and gave me resolve to finish what I'd begun.

Level your thinking. Don't get too excited about the victories or too discouraged with the defeats. And know that the challenges you are dealing with today are teaching you lessons that will allow your success tomorrow.

Yours,

Henry Ford

Henry Ford

"Luck is not chance—it's toil.
Fortune's expensive smile
is earned."

Emily Dickinson

Napoleon Bonaparte

"EMPEROR"

...was responsible for conquering the larger part of Europe. Napoleon was the greatest military genius of the nineteenth century.

1769–1821

It may seem odd to include a man like Napoleon in this book. After all, his very name is synonymous with the word "Dictator." In fact, he was thought in many circles to be the Antichrist of Revelation. Not exactly a role model for your teenager. So why is he here? Because I believe there had to be something, some very powerful force that drove a man like Napoleon Bonaparte; something that helped him overcome incredible odds, win over friend and foe alike, and ultimately, to change his world.

He was born and reared in Corsica. When his family fled to France early in his life, Napoleon was sent to military school. There he found his calling: to be a soldier. He became a general at the incredible age of twenty-four and from there started a march that would take him to the pinnacle of leadership in France—and then the whole world. Under his control, France became a leader in education, the arts, and even in the basic human rights we hold dear in America today, such as voting and freedom of religion.

What drove this unique combination of passionate social reformer and relentless warrior? Maybe that's the Napoleon Bonaparte we can find here. Maybe the thing that helped this man rule his world not only once, but twice, can help us through our own storms of perfection.

★ ★ ★ ★ NAPOLEON BONAPARTE ★ ★ ★ ★

Mr. Andy Andrews
P.O. Box 2761
Gulf Shores, Alabama 36547

Monsieur Andrews,

Waterloo. It is amazing to moi that one silly little afternoon in Belgium has been used to sum up an entire lifetime. Mon Dieu! It is not as though I sat around on my derriere eating truffles and bonbons. I conquered most of ze world for heaven's sake! Am I remembered for any of this? Is my name listed among the great cultivators of art and education in ze history of Europe? A man of culture and refinement? Non! I am known as the short guy with ze funny chapeau, the one with ze enormous ego and ze itchy chest! In most of your pictures I look like an insane shoplifter—although I must say I greatly enjoyed my appearances in your Bugs Bunny cartoons. What a comic genius. I have even been named as the originator of your infamous "Napoleon Complex" or "short man's syndrome," the obnoxious use of power and bullying to make up for insecurity in one's diminutiveness. Ask anyone. I was a teddy bear of a guy! But Waterloo! Ask any schoolchild about my grand legacy and he will say the name of that accursed Belgian town. And what of the man who defeated me, the Lion of Britain, the Duke of Wellington? He has a beef dish named after him. It is one thing to be beaten by a man who has a country, or even a nice car as his namesake, but beef tips and a nice gravy? It is enough to make one sick.

I joke, Monsieur Andrews, but I do wish to set the record straight concerning my exploits and achievements in the name of France. It is my most sincere hope that your readers will see a life that goes beyond one battle, one setback. I hope they will see a life of perseverance against long and terrible odds, of claiming victory when all seems lost. And above all, of doing what seems right, despite the consequences. If a life such as this one was of defeat and despair, then I am truly a vanquished man.

One of the misconceptions about me was that I was French. In actuality, my family was from Corsica, an island off the coast of Italy. My father was a tireless worker for the cause of Corsican independence, and after the French occupied Corsica, he became a French count. This enabled me to be educated at the École Militaire, from which I graduated in 1785 at the age of sixteen. The military at that time was an institution built on position and privilege. You can imagine the obstacles I faced, the discrimination aligned against a non-Frenchman. But one fateful day in 1793, I received the vindication my hard work and natural talents called for.

It was the time of the French Revolution, and I was lieutenant colonel in an artillery unit surrounding the port city of Toulon. With the aid of a British fleet, Toulon had defined the revolution. In answer to this recalcitrant attitude, our cannon took up positions around the city. A fierce battle began and my general was wounded. Taking command, I drove the British fleet from the harbor and took the city. For this I was made a brigadier general. Not bad for a short, balding twenty-four-year-old. I was a hero of all of France. I followed this victory with another that saved the government of France itself. A mob had formed in Paris, part of the murder and chaos that the revolution had become. My cannons were responsible for dispersing this maddened crowd when they attacked the ruling body. Again, I had saved my nation. This drove me even harder, as I determined that the name of Napoleon would forever be remembered as one of the giants in French lore! Or at least as the most famous guy under 5-foot-6.

In 1796, I became the commander of all French armies in Italy and conquered her. At least the northern half. Not satisfied, I then added Egypt to my possessions. The British rudely sank the fleet which was to return my army to France, so I settled in and reformed the Egyptian government. I had learned from the French Revolution the importance of the individual freedom of man. I made it a point from that time forward to insure that each nation that I conquered instituted reforms to grant these basic rights. In

Egypt, this meant ridding the country of an antiquated feudal system that made virtual slaves of most of the population. I know this predilection for freedom sounds odd from a man with a reputation for conquest, but every nation I brought under my rule emerged a more beneficent and free state than before. My goal was never subjugation but rather liberation, and I think I accomplished this goal to a great degree.

In 1799, I decided the government of France had become too weak to face her enemies. My colleagues and I thus formed the Consulate, with me as First Consul, of course. Later, in 1804, I felt Emperor had more of a ring to it and crowned myself with that title. And I continued to win on the battlefield as well, almost always against superior odds. My armies marched through Spain, Portugal, most of the Slavic nations, Poland, Prussia, and Holland, destroying any army placed in their path. But my victories were not solely on the battlefield. At home I restructured the government, wrote a new constitution guaranteeing voting rights and religious freedom to all men and granting them equality before the law. I created universities that were open to all students, regardless of their background. I created a system of laws, the Napoleonic Code, which influences the laws of Europe to this day. Scholars and scientists were given incomes and freedom to invent and create. France flourished as never before or since as the world's leading center in the arts and sciences.

But this magnificent era of progress was short-lived. In 1810, I made one of the saddest decisions of my life when I divorced the love of my life, the beautiful and delicate Josephine, to marry the daughter of the Emperor of Austria. It was a plan born of political pragmatism; I hoped that a child from such a union would be accepted throughout Europe as a legitimate ruler, but this was not the case. My heart never truly recovered, and I know Josephine was never the same. This, above all, remains my greatest regret, and my greatest blunder. It also was the beginning of the end of my dreams for France.

In 1812, I marched against a former ally, Alexander I of Russia.

From a military standpoint, my armies conquered as before. But the Russians burned everything in my path, until we faced the brutal Russian winter in Moscow with depleted supplies and no hope. I lost one quarter of my proud forces in retreat from that awful place. All of Europe sensed my weakness and rallied against me. My armies fought on, outnumbered and exhausted. Finally, in 1814, my generals had seen enough. They laid down their arms and pushed for peace. The allies refused to recognize my son as France's new ruler. I was forced into exile on the island of Elba in the Mediterranean. The dream was dead, and the most powerful man in French history was off the world stage. I could have died there, my friend. My armies no longer held continents in fear. No one heeded my orders. My wife and child were taken from me back to Austria. I was truly alone. I can tell you honestly that there is no worse feeling for a man of action than to be relegated to this nothing existence. To sit idly and watch the nation I formed being degraded by others was more than anyone could take. As with anyone in my predicament, I had two choices: fight or die. As you may have surmised, there was no choice. I escaped Elba and set sail for my beloved France. An army, the same army that I had led across the expanse of Europe, was now sent to arrest me and send be back to the godforsaken island. That I could not allow. I had always been a formidable advocate, but that day, I outshone my finest efforts. I poured out my heart. I poured out my dreams. By the end of that day, the army sent to imprison me was again under my command. We marched to Paris in triumph. My dark night, and that of France, was over. I could dream again.

As you know from the historical accounts, my second administration as ruler of France lasted some one hundred days before meeting its end at Waterloo. Though the people of France urged me to fight on, I knew her once-proud armies could take no more. The Old Guard had fallen. So I once again surrendered my rule, and myself, to the British. Exile this time was permanent, on the island of St. Helena.

Monsieur Andrews, it is no secret that in my life I was a proud, indeed vain man. My ego at times knew no bounds. But this same stubborn pride took me to heights my physical stature would never reach. It brought me back from the nightmare of exile, and allowed me to lead an army one last time. There are many things in life I regret, as do we all. But that proud day when the army of France marched again in triumph vindicated me. Never surrender.

Adieu,

Napoleon Bonaparte

David Livingstone

"MISSIONARY / DOCTOR"

…considered one of the most important explorers of Africa. Many of his maps are still in use today.

1813–1873

David Livingstone existed as a child in what would now be termed a "sweat shop." He grew up working hard and knew no other way of life. Livingstone's existence while growing up was one which would appall us today. The hardships of his young life groomed him to long for a higher purpose. He was a devoutly religious young man who gave his life over to the purpose of meeting the medical and spiritual needs of the natives in Africa. In this quest he also became a notable explorer.

Dr. David Livingstone is credited with some of the earliest discoveries on the continent of Africa while exploring its vastness in search of the needy. His explorations resulted in a revision of all contemporary maps of the African interior. He was a dedicated missionary and medical professional who won over the hearts of the societies of the West. His selfless commitment to the people of Africa brought him many miseries while suffering with diseases, hostile tribes, and a never-ending shortage of proper supplies. Dr. Livingstone's storms of perfection brought a season of prosperity and hope for many people.

DAVID LIVINGSTONE

Mr. Andy Andrews
P.O. Box 2761
Gulf Shores, Alabama 36547

Dear Mr. Andrews,

As a lad in Scotland, I grew up under fairly harsh conditions. Times were financially tough in my family, so I went to work at the age of ten. I worked as a "piecer" in the mill to help make ends meet, as did many other children. The typical workday was from six in the morning till eight at night, with half an hour for breakfast and half an hour for lunch: a workday of thirteen hours, six days a week. As a piecer, my job was to piece together threads on the spinning frame if they looked like they were breaking. This was vital, for unless flaws were detected early on, they were incorporated into the finished yard. Piecers needed sharp eyes and the power of constant attention if we were to avoid frequent beatings. We also had to be unusually agile since our work often involved climbing under the machinery or balancing over it. We often walked up to twenty miles a day in the mills, and much of this distance was covered by crawling or stooping. This often resulted in workers having bow legs and varicose veins.

By the end of the working day, most piecers were too tired to play, much less be in any frame of mind to learn. However, there were a handful of us who were tough and defied aching and tired limbs. We would make our way to the company school to spend two hours (8-10 p.m.) learning to read and write. Only about ten percent of my peers ever achieved any degree of literacy. My father was self-educated and had a great admiration for learning. He taught me to read and write; therefore I could start Latin during my first year of evening school. This would later benefit me when I decided to enter medical training. Between working long hours and going to school, there was no time for boyhood playtime. My reputation was that of an overearnest boy, exceptional not for my intelligence but for my obsessive determination to learn.

As a teen, I would roam the neighboring countryside, studying rocks and trees, and bring home plants and herbs to identify. I developed an interest in science which didn't exactly coincide with my dad's very strict religious beliefs. He believed science was ungodly. However, through contemporary readings and awareness of a religious revival taking place in Scotland, my dad's views changed through the years.

At twenty-one, I was still working in the mills, with no hope of freedom. I expressed an interest in medicine, but my father made it clear that he would oppose any medical training unless I put it to a specifically religious end. Medical missionaries were a comparatively new phenomenon . . . the answer to my dream. Medical school was now a reality.

While in medical school I suffered badly from inflammation of the bowels; however, I was determined not to let anything get in the way of my goals. I continued to attend classes even when I was not physically well. There were times I would have to walk through snowstorms, but I did not want to miss a lecture. I had saved money for a year and a half to get there; I couldn't give up now. While studying medicine, I also attended theology lectures and Greek classes. I had set my goals and spent my time doing the activities that were required to achieve those goals. Time for play was an unaffordable luxury.

As I was finishing my education, I started focusing on where I would put my talents to work. China had been of great interest to me, so I decided to pursue medical/missions work there. However, the Opium War broke out between Britain and China, and Britain decided that sending any more missionaries to China would be too risky. I had to change directions and find another place where I could make a difference. Africa it would be.

As you know, my life work was spent in Africa. I am noted for having explored and discovered a great majority of the lands of Africa. I was a medical missionary trying to help the people of this nation. I'm sure you have heard, "Dr. Livingstone, I presume?"—the most famous quote in regards to my life.

My times in Africa were extraordinary, but I came through tough times and trying conditions. The successes were born of many obstacles including detours, delays, malaria, and other illnesses, tsetse fly, slow and expensive transport, impassable swamps, political adversaries, and oftentimes death. Because of the obstacles, discoveries were made. Many times we have destination in mind, but God has other ideas that send us to other destinations—the right destination. Haven't you ever prayed for something, only to discover that God's answer was quite different than you expected?

I have told you tales of my boyhood in order to put into perspective my less-than-perfect circumstances. Learning to work hard and setting solid goals for yourself often will be the difference between success and failure in your life. Never give up on yourself or others. With hard work, determination, and help from God, success will be a reality. As I told some children in Scotland: Fear God, and work hard!

God Bless You,

David Livingstone
David Livingstone

"I know of no such unquestionable badge
and ensign of a sovereign mind
as that of tenacity of purpose."

Ralph Waldo Emerson

Martha Washington

"FIRST LADY"

...wife of the first president of the United States. During her husband's presidency, she was often called Lady Washington.

1732–1802

Martha Washington's personality has been eclipsed in history by the overwhelming fame of her husband, George. A perusal of her letter should reveal to us all the sacrifices she made in her personal life, and what freedoms we might not have enjoyed were it not for her graceful and dignified character in support of not only her husband, but of the United States of America as well.

We are all proud of our national flag. It inspires patriotism and lifts our spirits. But that strong pillar, the flagpole, which holds up Old Glory in all manner of foul weather, in daylight or darkness, in the midst of battle or over the honored cemetery, is often not noticed. Such an analogy is fitting to our original first lady. She was the worthy partner of the worthiest of men.

MARTHA WASHINGTON

Mr. Andy Andrews
P.O. Box 2761
Gulf Shores, Alabama 36547

Dear Mr. Andrews,

It has been nearly two hundred years since I left the stage of human affairs. Oh, what a joy it is for me to see that the red, white, and blue still flies (albeit with several more stars now) over the blessed United States of America! Such precarious situations, decisions, and delicate scales seem to hold the destiny of mankind. I understand, more so now than ever, that a True Master determines the course of our world regardless of how self-important we pretend to be. Nevertheless, while exercising our own free will, we can either fulfill great callings or hinder them as we use or abuse our gifts of character.

Prior to meeting my beloved George, I was already well acquainted with trials and adversity. Although I had been born and raised in a dignified family in the British colony of Virginia, with a circle of influence and financial means, I discovered that the falling of misfortune does not discriminate along financial lines. George was not my first husband. Indeed, I had been left widowed with two surviving children of the four I had given birth to when my path crossed that of Colonel George Washington.

The loss of a husband and two children, whom I dearly loved, was a crushing blow to me. Our medical knowledge wasn't the tenth of what it is now, and no remedies were then known for ailments which now are commonly taken lightly. I was but twenty-four years old and felt that I had no hope left for happiness. I realized much later that this affliction was a proving ground for later trials which would have outcomes much more far reaching than one single family. I was forced to either become strong or abandon all hope. I found that I could not abandon hope while I still had my two remaining children. With a courage which can only be forged in the fire of such distress, I became strong and developed a strength of dignity and character which I had occasion to draw upon many times later.

The courtship between George and me was a whirlwind. After only four encounters together, I accepted his proposal of marriage. He was a stunning man of stature and of personality, a war hero for the British army. He was a promising man, who intended to resign from the army and to farm at his home of Mount Vernon. Although Mount Vernon was far from my remaining family, I was happy to follow him there with the promise of beginning a real family life again. It was so important to me to have him for my husband and father to my children. I needed the security of such surroundings. It was my dream.

George found himself more and more frustrated with the British army, and England generally. He had resigned from the army, and I finally began realizing my hopes of the family life I had always dreamed of. But George, being well known across the colonies for his valor in war, was among a large company of like-minded and learned men who saw the protective hand of England becoming an oppressive claw of domination. The situation grew much worse over the period of years, and small-scale rebellions began breaking out in the colonies. The Boston Tea Party was a fulcrum used for England's heavy-handedness. The colonists began looking to George, their beloved war hero of the colonies, for guidance. He would know what they should do. I feared for my husband and my family.

Franklin, Jefferson, Adams, Hancock, and many others helped shape the colonists' resolve. I knew all too well that if a revolution were to take place, my George would be called upon to act as the commander in chief of the American army. But what of my desires? My dreams were important, too! This would mean losing him to a war likely to be waged for years, and the possibility of losing him forever. George was known for great gallantry in the face of fire, and very few soldiers with such boldness survived long in war.

I also knew, however, that no matter the cost, George would not decline the position. He could not. He would be less of a man, and not the man I had grown to love if he surrendered to my repetitive protests toward him for considering such a task. I therefore chose to leave the decision entirely up to him. I knew he loved me, and that it would pain him greatly to cause me such sorrow. I need not burden him even more so. My husband was a warrior, the finest and most gallant in the land. America needed such a man. Destiny was calling for the both of us, and for America herself. I reluctantly set aside my dreams of having a family with my husband at home and the secure routine born of such comforts.

The shot heard round the world was fired near Concord, Massachusetts. Soon thereafter my husband left me for the clash of arms, the spilling of blood, the explosion of cannons, the beat of the drums, and the lonely whisperings of the fife. After he left me, I cried for hours. Would I ever have my husband back for myself again; for just me and our family? Would my children ever know a normal life? Would I find the happiness of a reunion with my husband, or again feel the knife's blade at my heart when I heard the news of his death. Was I destined for a life of bereavement? I felt guilty at times for such selfish thoughts, when so many others were giving everything they had for the endeavor against the tyrannical British. But I could not help it. Life was not fair!

Eight years of worry, bloodshed, fear, dread, and hope accompanied the Revolutionary War. I was able to see George on frequent occasions during this time, but never without the concern that it would be for the last time. Meanwhile, my children were growing up. Indeed, my son was nearly a grown man now. What had happened to my hopes? My hopes had changed during this time, but I found happiness and pride in what my husband stood for. I also found that what I felt about the war also had a great impact on others, both men and women. Victory at long last brought my husband home to me, but he was there for only four short years before he was duty bound to leave me again.

After the war, George retired from public life and refused the numerous pleas of the populace to take political positions in the new republic. I was so happy. My son was grown and started a family of his own, while I finally had my husband for myself. Was it too late to start the dream again? But alas, without a strong constitution, and with the current weakness of the Articles of Confederation, the newly founded United States of America was falling to pieces amidst state rivalries and a bitter north versus south mindset.

A new continental congress had to be seated in order to prevent the new union from dissolving so soon, and after such a hard-won victory of independence. George, of course, was summoned. And, of course, he could not decline. He left Mount Vernon for Philadelphia, where the Continental Congress adopted the plan of a two-chambered congress, a court of last resort, and a chief executive officer to guide the country under the direction of the constitution. Although it was not a perfect system of government, its system strengthened the weaknesses of the Articles of Confederation and appeared to be the relief the country needed. I knew all too well that George, the most popular man in America, would be the obvious choice to fulfill the capacity of "President."

This inevitability came to pass. George again was leaving Mount Vernon in order to hold the position of the President of the United States of America. It was a position he had desperately hoped to avoid. He was sincere in his wish to retire from public life and give himself entirely to me, as he knew I most desired. He could not, however, decline what he knew to be his duty when the country was in such desperate need of strong leadership. George left for New York while I stayed behind and cried again. Eventually, I accompanied him for his eight-year obligation as the president.

At the conclusion of George's presidency, we did go back to Mount Vernon. A long time delayed, but we did find the total contentedness with our own togetherness. And Mount Vernon was never a lonely place. It was continually filled with statesmen and family who stayed months or even years at a time. It was my dream. I was happy, and more so because of the difficulties to which we were subject during our years of marriage. Had I received what I immediately wanted in the beginning, or followed my personal desire to dissuade my husband from his duty for my own selfish dreams, neither I nor perhaps thousands of free Americans later would have enjoyed the supreme measure of happiness which I ultimately came to know.

I learned that in giving of yourself and in sacrificing immediate gain for distant investment, much greater good will come than otherwise. Over many years, the status of my husband and me has been raised almost to nobility. If only our English forefathers could have recognized that nobility is not a birthright! Nobility is earned, and defined by one's character. Such nobility has been displayed by many Americans, the least of which has been displayed by me. May God continue to bless the United States of America!

In God We Trust,

Martha Washington

1774–1809   *1770–1838*

Meriwether Lewis & William Clark

"EXPLORERS"

…mapped the land of the Louisiana Purchase.
Their expedition was crucial to opening the West for settlement.

What if a friend of yours bought some land and asked you to look it over for him? What if you found out that the land stretched some 2,000 miles, all the way to the Pacific Ocean? That was the challenge facing Meriwether Lewis and William Clark: to explore the land of the Louisiana Purchase. They were to be explorers and mapmakers of the territory; scientists studying the plants and animals; diplomats befriending the people they met; and soldiers defending this new frontier. Sounds easy, doesn't it?

With this mission ahead of them, Lewis and Clark set out from St. Louis with a contingent of fifty men, plenty of supplies, and some big dreams. Along the way, they would face diseases, savage storms, raging rivers, wild animals, frostbite, starvation, and hostile Indians. But they never stopped moving forward until they heard the roar of the waves and became the first Americans to see the Pacific Ocean. Their exploration paved the way for the great western migration that transformed our country from a collection of coastal states into a vast and powerful nation. See what two men, courage, and a consistent effort can accomplish?

LEWIS & CLARK

Mr. Andy Andrews
P.O. Box 2761
Gulf Shores, Alabama 36547

Dear Mr. Andrews,

How I wish you could see this. I myself have seen an ocean before, but this one is on the other end of a continent from the one to which I am accustomed. It is the Pacific, and for the next winter, it will be our home. I wish I could say it was a hospitable neighbor, but I would be lying if I said such a thing. We have built a stockade here and named it Fort Clatsop, after the local Indians, but it is little protection against the constant wind, rain, and sea spray. The constant cold and rain may have dampened our clothing, but not our spirits. We have achieved our goal. We have traveled to the farthest reaches of our fledgling nation. No longer are we a small collection of states huddled along the eastern shore. Our country now stretches from one sea to the next. America may now begin to take her place among the great powers of the world.

I wish I could also say in all honesty that the journey across this vast land was an easy one. It was not. Along our way we encountered obstacles as varied as storms, Indians, wild animals, and frostbite. The fierce river rapids we faced very nearly destroyed our boats and canoes on more than one occasion. In fact, only two months into the mission we encountered a sudden, violent squall so powerful that it nearly sank our fifty-five-foot keelboat and sent our two smaller craft half a mile downstream. Had it not been for the courageous actions of the crew, the expedition would most probably have had to be forfeited.

Let us say a word about the forty-three brave men and one Indian woman who make up the life-blood of this undertaking. They have performed their duties with honor and distinction. Their discipline in the toughest of situations has saved our lives more times than we can recall. Without them, there would be no expedition. I am proud to have commanded them.

Despite the great perils and hardships that we have faced, we have lost only one man, Sgt. Floyd, who succumbed to appendicitis early in the journey. May his soul rest in peace.

This is the second winter we have faced since our departure from St. Louis in May 1804. It was our first winter that forced us to face the possibility that we may never see our goal of the Pacific Ocean. We had encountered numerous tribes during our travels, some hostile, but most willing to trade with us. They seemed to be most impressed with our slave, York, as they realized that the black on York's skin would simply not rub off. However, the long journey and numerous tribes soon depleted our supply of gifts, and we began to run out of items to trade for food. The situation became so tenuous at one point that we began to be known as "the dog-eaters" because that was all we had to eat.

It was the Mandan tribe that saved us that winter. Their gifts of buffalo meat and the buffalo hides that came with them enabled us to stave off the bitter cold we were forced to endure. Before this time, we had begun to think that there was no way we could ask our men to go through this brutal climate. We had pondered whether we could indeed tame such a harsh country. But we reasoned that we had survived the very most this land could throw at us, and it was with a newfound resolve to achieve our goals that we pushed on to the Pacific Northwest.

We had been bowed, but not broken. In our minds, we had won. We exchanged our tattered, rotting clothing with which we had begun our trip for the buckskin of our Indian companions. And in late March, when the thaws came, we pointed our canoes again westward, to the Pacific Ocean.

And that is why we can address you today from this place—because our dogged determination and our will to succeed were greater forces than even the worst nature could throw at us. We pray that your readers may benefit from our experience. Our experience, of course, is the endurance of prolonged struggle. The more we struggled, the stronger we became. The struggle developed muscles, so to speak, and because of our strength of character, will, and physicality—victory was inevitable. So our advice is to struggle. When you do, whole new worlds will open up before your eyes.

Godspeed,

Meriwether Lewis & William Clark

"In lowliness of mind let each esteem
others better than himself. Let each of you
look out not only for his own interests,
but also for the interests of others."

Philippians 2:3-4

Isaac Newton

"MATHEMATICIAN/ PHYSICIST"

...developed the calculus. From his three laws of motion, he derived the Law of Universal Gravitation.

1642–1727

Some of us had a tough time with high school algebra, therefore Isaac Newton remains to us "the guy who got hit on the head by an apple." The relationships of tangents, curves, and their inverse operations, however, are the parameters that framed much of Newton's early success. They led to the discovery of his "fluxional method" and were the basis of his development of calculus.

Isaac Newton was one of the greatest scientists of history, who made important contributions to many fields of science. His discoveries and theories laid the foundation for much of the progress in science since his time. Newton is probably best known for discovering universal gravitation—the apple on the head—which explains that all bodies in space and on earth are affected by the force called gravity. In addition to this, Newton made profound discoveries related to the science of dynamics and the laws of motion.

Though his talents and mental capacities were certainly extraordinary, Isaac Newton shared the basic and common hardships associated with adversity, rejection, and disappointment.

Isaac Newton

Mr. Andy Andrews
P.O. Box 2761
Gulf Shores, Alabama 36547

I welcome the opportunity to contact you via this missive. Perhaps you already know that I am a well-known man of science.

One of my most famous contributions was the invention of the branch of mathematics called calculus. I also helped solve the mysteries of light and optics, and I derived the law of universal gravitation—what is often referred to as the law of gravity.

At the time of my work, these developments were entirely new and were greeted with astonishment and admiration by most of my colleagues. Thus one might think that I would be a happy man, always praised and lauded. But such was not the case. One very sad element present in my life was competition from those who were simply envious, or who sincerely felt that their own discoveries preceded mine or were superior to mine.

I can't tell you how disheartening such incidents were. One such case involved the German scientist Leibniz, who claimed priority in the invention of calculus. Nothing could be further from the truth. It was I who was first. I fought for my rights and accused him of plagiarism. Sadly, there resulted a lifelong quarrel between Leibniz and me.

In another instance, in order for my studies in astronomy to be perfected, I required access to observations of John Flamsteed, the first Astronomer Royal of England. But Flamsteed was uncooperative, and this matter led to a painful conflict.

Perhaps the most painful incident was when I myself was accused of plagiarism by the English philosopher and physicist Robert Hooke, who claimed that I had stolen from him a central idea regarding universal gravitation. I went through a miserable period during which I claimed, rightfully, that the ideas in my book, *The Principia,* belonged solely to me. Although most historians came to accept my innocence in the case, it was terribly painful to live through.

You must bear in mind that I was always a very shy and private person. So you can imagine my dismay, to be accused publicly of the above crimes, knowing all along that I was honest.

And because publication of *The Principia* created a furor, in a positive way, indeed marking a turning point in the history of science, I was never again to feel myself a private person. I now came to enjoy, or suffer, one of the accoutrements of fame, namely, constant public notice.

So you can see that there were severe stresses in my life, when I would have been content to placidly and quietly pursue my discoveries. In some cases, I even kept my discoveries to myself, rather than publish them and risk painful criticism.

Over time, these things have a way of piling up. I ultimately suffered a severe emotional disorder. Oh, I recovered my health, but my creative days were finished.

How was I to save myself from these inordinate stresses? In my later years, I devoted myself to the study of theology—God, in His various manifestations—quietly withdrawing into myself. Fortunately, in spite of the animosity that had been generated by the various clashes described, I had many good friends who stood by me and were a comfort to me. I was now a famous and respected man. Many artists painted my portrait. I also gave to charity, to aid those less fortunate than myself.

So, my later days being filled with quiet and contemplation, I at last achieved the peace I had always wanted. I don't know what I may seem to the world, but to myself, I seem to have been only like a boy playing on the seashore, diverting myself and now and then finding a smoother pebble or a prettier shell than ordinary, while the great ocean of truth lay undiscovered before me.

Most respectfully, I am your servant,

Is. Newton
Isaac Newton

Michelangelo

"SCULPTOR/ ARCHITECT/ ARTIST"

… is best known for his work in the Sistine Chapel. He was one of the most inspired creators in the history of art.

1475–1564

Michelangelo, the legendary painter, architect, sculptor, and poet, was a great leader of the Italian Renaissance. Famous for countless works, including the statue of David, the artist was known for his trademark style of showcasing the extremes of heroism and tragedy. A disciple of the sculptor Donatello, Michelangelo soon stopped painting to concentrate on sculpture, an art form that enabled him to better exhibit the force and movement that were unique to his style.

After moving from Rome to Florence in 1501, he met Leonardo da Vinci, and soon the two were commissioned by the new democratic regime to create great battle scenes for the walls of the city hall. Leonardo is credited with teaching Michelangelo the secret of making movement appear both flowing and vibrant.

Although the painting of the ceiling of the Sistine Chapel in the Vatican is his most famous work, Michelangelo is also well known for his marble sculpture *Pieta*, which shows the Virgin Mary cradling the dead Jesus after the Crucifixion, and his frescoes *The Crucifixion of Saint Peter* and *The Conversion of Saint Paul*, both commissioned by Pope Paul III.

MR. ANDY ANDREWS
P.O. BOX 2761
GULF SHORES, ALABAMA 36547

MY DEAR YOUNG MAN,

PLEASE DO NOT THINK ME UNWILLING TO OFFER YOU AND YOUR READERS A SMALL WINDOW INTO MY SOUL. IN SPITE OF THE LATE HOUR AT WHICH I COMPLETE THIS LETTER, IT IS MY HOPE THAT YOU WILL ACCEPT IT NONETHELESS. MY TARDINESS IS QUITE SIMPLY A RESULT OF MY PREOCCUPATION WITH THE WORK AT HAND, THE PAINTING OF THE GREAT VAULT IN THE SISTINE CHAPEL IN THE VATICAN. IT IS A COMMISSION I ACCEPTED FROM HIS HOLINESS, POPE JULIUS II, ON THIS VERY DATE FOUR YEARS AGO.

I HAD ALWAYS THOUGHT OF ROME AS A BROAD FIELD IN WHICH A MAN MAY DEMONSTRATE HIS WORTH. HOWEVER, SOON AFTER MY ARRIVAL IN 1496, I BECAME TROUBLED BY THE MATERIALISM I WITNESSED. FIVE YEARS LATER, AT THE AGE OF TWENTY-SIX, I MOVED BACK TO FLORENCE, WHERE I WAS TRULY APPRECIATED. THE NEW GOVERNMENT WISHED TO DISPLAY THE TALENTS OF ITS TWO PREEMINENT ARTISTS—ME AND A THEN NEW ACQUAINTANCE OF MINE, LEONARDO DA VINCI. ALTHOUGH I LEARNED FROM LEONARDO, HE AND I BECAME RIVALS FOR THE AFFECTIONS OF THE PATRONS.

IN 1505, POPE JULIUS CALLED ME BACK TO ROME. EVER SINCE, WE HAVE CARRIED ON A TEMPERAMENTAL, IRKSOME RELATIONSHIP. I FEAR THAT IN MY ZEAL FOR CREATING GRAND WORKS IN STONE, I ACCEPTED JULIUS'S COMMISSION FOR A PROJECT TOO VAST, A LARGE SEPULCHRE CONTAINING MORE THAN FORTY LIFE-SIZE MARBLE FIGURES. HIS HOLINESS BELIEVES IT WILL SOMEDAY BE CONSIDERED THE EIGHTH WONDER OF THE WORLD. SIX LABORIOUS YEARS LATER, I SIMPLY WONDER IF I WILL EVER COMPLETE IT. I HAVE ENDURED PROBLEMS WITH QUARRYING, INADEQUATE FINANCING, UNRELIABLE ASSISTANTS, AND CONSTANT PAPAL TANTRUMS. FOLLOWING A PARTICULARLY INSULTING AFFRONT, I FLED ON HORSEBACK, RETURNING TO FLORENCE ONCE AGAIN.

SEVEN MONTHS LATER, I FOUND MYSELF AT HIS FEET, HUMBLING MYSELF IN AN EFFORT TO EFFECT A RECONCILIATION. AFTER EXECUTING A BRONZE STATUE OF JULIUS, I RECEIVED THE FIRST PAYMENT TO BEGIN MY WORK ON THE SISTINE CHAPEL.

I was most unhappy that day in May of 1508 when I embarked on this herculean task. I, Michelangelo, a great and renowned sculptor, was being forced to paint instead of sculpt.

My first concern was the construction of a scaffold from which to paint a ceiling fifty feet high. After some unsuccessful attempts, I devised a rather ingenious keystone arch system whose structure would leave the chapel available for services. I must climb steep ladders each day to reach this very uncomfortable place from which I paint.

Another challenge for me was putting up with Julius's unimaginative plan for the paintings. I proceeded with *my* interpretation. He later complained that the work was progressing too slowly. He also ridiculed the absence of real gold in my painting. I replied, "The prophets I have painted were poor men; they had no gold."

Further hampering the project was my unfamiliarity with the fresco technique, so I sent to Florence for a number of proficient collaborators. Their work proved to be disappointingly inadequate, so I sent them away. I drew upon all of my inner strength, scraped away the painting the others had done, and set about the painting of the Great Flood with only my pigment-grinder at my side.

But just halfway through, my colors mildewed and blistered, leaving my figures almost unrecognizable. I was distraught. Did I not explain to the pope that painting was not my profession? I beseeched him to find someone to advise me on proper technique, and then I locked myself in the chapel, never again allowing anyone to interfere with my work on the vault.

It is certain that there have been many other challenges during this project, in specific, and in my life, in general. And if I am fortunate enough to live a long and productive life, there will be new challenges, I am sure. Although I began this enormous painting with grave doubts that I could accomplish it, I have become immersed in the raptures of creation itself and have come to know that nothing is impossible.

I must bid you farewell to return to my high perch and pigments. I shall finish my work here in a few months—and then on to new challenges.

Your servant,

MICHELANGELO

"Let us not grow weary while doing good,
for in due season we shall reap
if we do not lose heart."

Galatians 6:9

Will Rogers

"AUTHOR/ HUMORIST"

...achieved worldwide fame through his humorous monologues and rope tricks.

1879–1935

There is a lot to be said for the philosophies and insights of an old cowboy. Will Rogers came from a quieter time and an era where common sense still seemed the norm. He was a romantic, whose down-home country wisdom was easily accepted because of his witty but sincere delivery toward politics, social issues, and general life in America. It was hard to argue with his salient points, especially the ones made while trick roping! He put a spin on the facts of life while making your side ache with laughter.

It is hard to describe in specifics just what Will Rogers was. He was an entertainer of course, but more than that. Will Rogers was a philosopher. He was perhaps the forerunner to other modern American sages such as Erma Bombeck. He was respected and admired by political figures across America, and was a beloved social hero who captured the affections of the nation with his hat-in-hand humility and homespun outlook on our society.

Mr. Andy Andrews
P.O. Box 2761
Gulf Shores, Alabama 36547

Dear Andy,

Shucks, what an honor to be included in your book! Ain't this a
great country, where a man can say what's on his mind, poke fun
at politicians, and find humor in situations that ain't so funny—
and get away with it! (See . . . I must have gotten away with it . . .
you invited me here today!)

If you want to look at yourself and wonder how in the world you
turned out the way you did, look back. Look back at your family;
look back at your circumstances; and look back at events that
have taken place in your life. How'd ya handle them?

My dad was not only a rancher, businessman, and cattleman; he
also was influential in the politics of the Cherokee Nation. (I'm
part Cherokee, you know.) He was known as a hard bargainer,
but always fair. Living in a rural community, Dad gave me a
horse I learned to ride; and I learned trick roping at a very early
age—and loved it. This would be the beginning of my entertainment career. Dad being in politics made me aware of what's
going on in the world, past my front porch. Soon I found out I
had an opinion about goings-on in this world and like to share my
opinions. Can you see it coming?

Mom was loved by all; she was a missionary for the poor and for those in any kind of difficulty. She spoke with a soft voice, displayed good manners, and had a calm demeanor and a wonderful sense of humor. I'd like to say that I inherited some of her better qualities. She died when I was twelve, and it was the saddest time of my life.

I was a terrible student growing up. Of course, you can normally figure that out by just listening to me talk, or trying to read my writing. My parents couldn't keep me focused on school work; was more interested in lassoing the kids in the schoolyard and doing my rope tricks than any learning to be done. I won't even begin to tell you how many schools I was in and out of! Proper grammar and punctuation were never my best qualities . . . isn't it funny that in my later writings, these are what became my trademark.

I started traveling with the Wild West shows and circuses as a serious trick roper—finally was doing what I loved best in life. Between tricks or after misses, I'd notice folks laughing, and I didn't like that at all. No sir. Thought they was laughing *at* me. Instead I found they was laughing *with* me. I'd be making common sense observations about life here in the United States, and was soon pegged as Will Rogers, the humorist, social critic, political observer, and maybe even philosopher. How 'bout that for an old country boy?

I was living in a time when millions of unemployed Americans were enduring tough times during this country's most serious crisis since the Civil War. I found that a smile had disappeared from the lips of America and her eyes were filled with tears. I found that poking fun at the pompous politicians, self-righteous educators and religious leaders, crooked corporate executives, communism, or whatever helped ease some of the pain. I tried to make you laugh at these absurdities, seeing the frauds for what they were—never forgetting that politics are not all of life. I would like to point out here that no one was safe from my observations. Anyone was fair game! I would read the papers and magazines and then simply comment on what I had read in a manner easily understood by the common man through the use of humor—never through maliciousness.

HUMOR . . . laughing in the face of adversity rather than wallowing in the darkness of despair. There are so many difficult times we experience in life. By finding the humor, we often will recognize the idiocy of the situation and perhaps in doing so ease the pain. It's not enough just to grumble and complain when things are bad. You have to locate the source of the problem.

When I die, my epitaph, or whatever you call it—those signs on your gravestones—is gonna read: "I joked about almost every prominent man of my time but I never met one I didn't like!" I am so proud of that, I can hardly wait to die so it can be carved. And when you come around to my grave, I'll be sittin' there proudly reading it.

Thanks for listening . . . again!

Will Rogers

Will Rogers

Bibliography

Allan, Herbert, S. *John Hancock, Patriot in Purple*. New York: Macmillan, 1948.

Bartlett, Henry Leigh. *Beethoven—Democratic Friend*. San Antonio: The Naylor Company, 1973.

Binger, Carl. *Thomas Jefferson, A Well-Tempered Man*. New York: W. W. Norton, 1970.

Borough, James. *The Ford Dynasty: An American Story*. Garden City, N.Y.: Doubleday, 1977.

Brandes, George (trans. by Heinz Norden). *Michelangelo: His Life, His Times, His Era*. New York: Frederick Ungar, 1963.

Bubbeo, Daniel. *Humphrey Bogart, To Have and Have Not*. Internet access at http://www.macconsult.com/mikersoe/bogart/bio.html, 1997.

Carnegie, Andrew. *Autobiography of Andrew Carnegie*. Boston: Houghton Mifflin, 1948.

Churchill, Randolph S. *Winston Churchill* (vol. 1). Boston: Houghton Mifflin, 1966–1983.

Complete Works of William Shakespeare, The. New York: The World Syndicate Publishing Company, 1929.

Cook, Sir Edward. *The Life of Florence Nightingale*. New York: Macmillan, 1942.

Creamer, Robert W. *Babe: The Legend Comes to Life*. New York: Simon & Schuster, 1992.

Cunningham, Noble E., Jr. *In Pursuit of Reason: The Life of Thomas Jefferson*. Baton Rouge: Louisiana State University Press, 1987.

Dale Carnegie's Biographical Roundup, "Highlights in the Lives of Forty Famous People." Freeport, N.Y.: Books for Libraries Press, 1970.

De Madariaga, Salvador. *Hernán Cortés, Conqueror of Mexico*. Coral Gables: University of Miami Press, 1942.

Dyson, John, *Westward with Columbus*. New York: Simon & Schuster / Madison Press Book, 1991.

Elliot, Lawrence. "The Long Hunter." Reader's Digest Press. New York: Thomas Y. Cromwell, 1976.

Fantel, Hans. *William Penn, Apostle of Dissent*. New York.: William Morrow, 1974.

Fishwick, Marshall W. *Illustrious Americans: Clara Barton*. Morristown, N.J.: Silver Burdett, 1966.

Fitzpatrick, James K. *Builders of the American Dream*. New Rochelle: Arlington House, 1977.

Fleming, Thomas. *The Man from Monticello, An Intimate Life of Thomas Jefferson*. New York: William Morrow, 1969.

Foley, John P., ed. *The Jefferson Cyclopedia*. New York: Funk & Wagnall, 1900.

Franklin, Benjamin. *Benjamin Franklin: A Biography in His Own Words*. New York: Harper & Row, 1972.

Goldrosen, John. *The Buddy Holly Story*. Bowling Green, KY: Bowling Green University Press, 1975.

Guérard, Albert. *Napoleon I, A Great Life in Brief*. New York: Frederick Ungar, 1935.

Guillemin, Henri. *Joan, Maid of Orleans*. New York: Saturday Review Press, 1970.

Henderson, Archibald D. *Contemporary Immortals*. New York: Appleton, 1930.

Hesseltine, William B. *Ulysses S. Grant, Politician*. New York: Frederick Ungar, 1935.

Holloway, David. *Lewis & Clark and the Crossing of North America*. New York: Saturday Review Press, 1974.

Hyams, Joe. *Bogie: The Biography of Humphrey Bogart*. New York: The New American Library, 1996.

Jeal, Tim. *Livingstone*. New York: G. P. Putnam's Sons, 1973.

Josephson, Matthew. *Edison*. New York: McGraw-Hill, 1959.

Keller, Helen. *Teacher, Anne Sullivan Macy*. New York: Doubleday, 1956.

Kelly, Fred Chaters. *Miracle at Kittyhawk*. New York: Farrar, 1951.

Lester, David, and Irene Lester. *Ike and Mamie*. New York: G. P. Putnam's Sons, 1981.

Lingg, Ann M. *Mozart: Genius of Harmony*. New York: Henry Holt, 1949.

Mayo, Bernard, ed. *Jefferson Himself, The Personal Narrative of a Many-Sided American*. Boston: Houghton Mifflin, 1942.

McGhee, Richard D. *John Wayne: Actor, Artist, Hero*. Jefferson, N.C.: McFarland, 1990.

Miller, Russell. *The House of Getty*. New York: Henry Holt, 1985.

Morris, Bayard J. *Hernando Cortes: Five Letters*. New York: W. W. Norton, 1976.

Mosley, Leonard. *Lindbergh: A Biography*. Garden City, N.Y.: Doubleday, 1976.

Mossiker, Frances. *Pocahontas, The Life and Legend*. New York: Alfred A. Knopf, 1976.

Owens, Jesse (with Paul G. Neimark). *Blackthink: My Life as Black Man and White Man*. New York: William Morrow, 1970.

Payne, Robert. *By Me, William Shakespeare*. New York: Everest House, 1980.

Philip, Cynthia Owen. *Robert Fulton*. New York: Franklin Watts, 1985.

Phillips, Leon. *The First Lady of America: A Romanticized Biography of Pocahontas*. Richmond, Va.: Westover, 1973.

Randall, William Sterne. *Thomas Jefferson, A Life*. New York: Henry Holt, 1993.

Rawlins, Dennis. *Peary at the North Pole: Fact or Fiction?* New York: Robert B. Luce, 1973.

Reid, Robert. *Marie Curie*. Saturday Review Press. New York: E. P. Dutton, 1974.

Richards, Norman. *Dreamers & Doers: Inventors Who Changed Our World*. New York: Atheneum, 1984.

Robinson, Ray. *American Original: A Life of Will Rogers*. New York: Oxford University Press, 1996.

Rogers, Will. *The Autobiography of Will Rogers*. Boston: Houghton Mifflin, 1979.

Samborn, Margaret. *Robert E. Lee: The Complete Man*. Philadelphia: J. B. Rippincott,1967.

Schoor, Gene. *The Jim Thorpe Story: America's Greatest Athlete*. New York: Julian Messner, 1951.

Sherr, Lynn. *Failure Is Impossible: Susan B. Anthony in Her Own Words*. New York: Times Books (Div. of Random House), 1995.

Thane, Elswyth. *Washington's Lady*. New York: Dodd, Mead & Co., 1960.

Thayer, William Roscoe. *George Washington*. New York: Houghton Mifflin, 1922.

Thomas, Benjamin Platt. *Abraham Lincoln: Autobiography*. New York: Modern Library, 1952.

Thwaites, Reuben Gold. *Daniel Boone*. Williamstown, Mass.: Corner House, 1977.

Vallentin, Antonina. *Picasso*. London: Trinity, 1963.

Villiers, Alan. *Captain James Cook*. New York: Charles Scribner's Sons, 1967.

Wallace, Irving. *The Fabulous Showman: The Life & Times of P. T. Barnum*. New York: Alfred A. Knopf, 1959.

Washington, Booker T. *Up From Slavery*. Garden City, N.Y.: Doubleday, 1963.

Weems, John, *Peary: The Explorer and the Man*. Boston: Riverside Press Cambridge, 1976.

Westfall, Richard S. *The Life of Isaac Newton*. Cambridge:University Press, 1993.

ALPHABETICAL INDEX

For booking information,
additional copies of this series,
or to see other popular items by Andy Andrews
such as comedy cassettes, motivational tapes
and a variety of t-shirts, please call for a free color brochure.

1-800-726-ANDY
24 hours a day

or you may write to:

Andy Andrews
P.O. Box 17321
Nashville, TN 37217
USA
or
Visit Andy's Web Site At:
www.AndyAndrews.com